Enterprise Social for the Java Platform

Shares, Mashups, Likes, and Ways to Integrate Social Media into Your Cloud Native Enterprise Java Applications

Werner Keil

Apress®

Enterprise Social for the Java Platform: Shares, Mashups, Likes, and Ways to Integrate Social Media into Your Cloud Native Enterprise Java Applications

Werner Keil
Bad Homburg, Hessen, Germany

ISBN-13 (pbk): 978-1-4842-9570-0   ISBN-13 (electronic): 978-1-4842-9571-7
https://doi.org/10.1007/978-1-4842-9571-7

Managing Director, Apress Media LLC: Welmoed Spahr
Acquisitions Editor: Aditee Mirashi
Development Editor: James Markham
Coordinating Editor: Mark Powers

Cover designed by eStudioCalamar

Cover image by Nupo Deyon Daniel on Unsplash (www.unsplash.com)

Distributed to the book trade worldwide by Apress Media, LLC, 1 New York Plaza, New York, NY 10004, U.S.A. Phone 1-800-SPRINGER, fax (201) 348-4505, e-mail orders-ny@springer-sbm.com, or visit www.springeronline.com. Apress Media, LLC is a California LLC and the sole member (owner) is Springer Science + Business Media Finance Inc (SSBM Finance Inc). SSBM Finance Inc is a **Delaware** corporation.

For information on translations, please e-mail booktranslations@springernature.com; for reprint, paperback, or audio rights, please e-mail bookpermissions@springernature.com.

Apress titles may be purchased in bulk for academic, corporate, or promotional use. eBook versions and licenses are also available for most titles. For more information, reference our Print and eBook Bulk Sales web page at http://www.apress.com/bulk-sales.

Any source code or other supplementary material referenced by the author in this book is available to readers on GitHub (https://github.com/Apress). For more detailed information, please visit https://www.apress.com/gp/services/source-code.

Paper in this product is recyclable

This book is dedicated to my beautiful wife and my wonderful children, for their patience and understanding as well as giving me the energy and motivation to finish this book.

Table of Contents

About the Author

Werner Keil is a Cloud Native consultant, Jakarta EE and Microservice expert for the financial sector. He helps Global 500 enterprises across industries and leading IT vendors. He worked for over 30 years as IT manager, PM, coach, and SW architect and consultant for the finance, mobile, media, transport, and public sectors. Werner develops enterprise systems using Java, Java/Jakarta EE, Oracle, IBM, Spring or Microsoft technologies, JavaScript, Node.js, Angular, and dynamic or functional languages. He is a Committer at Apache Foundation and Eclipse Foundation, a Babel Language Champion, a UOMo Project Lead, and an active member of the Java Community Process in JSRs like 321 (Trusted Java), 344 (JSF 2.2), 354 (Money, also Maintenance Lead), 358/364 (JCP.next), 362 (Portlet 3), 363 (Unit-API 1), 365 (CDI 2), 366 (Java EE 8), 375 (Java EE Security), 380 (Bean Validation 2), and 385 (Unit-API 2, also Spec Lead), and was the longest serving Individual Member of the Executive Committee for nine years in a row until 2017. Werner is currently the Committer Member representative in the Jakarta EE Specification Committee. He was among the first five Jakarta EE Ambassadors when it was founded as Java EE Guardians and is a member of its leadership council.

About the Technical Reviewer

 **Reza Rahman** is Principal Program Manager for Java on Azure at Microsoft. He works to make sure Java developers are first class citizens at Microsoft and Microsoft is a first class citizen of the Java ecosystem.

Reza has been an official Java technologist at Oracle. He is the author of the popular book *EJB 3 in Action* from Manning Publications. Reza has long been a frequent speaker at Java User Groups and conferences worldwide including JavaOne and Devoxx. He has been the lead for the Java EE track at JavaOne as well as a JavaOne Rock Star Speaker award recipient. He was the program chair for the inaugural JakartaOne conference. Reza is an avid contributor to industry journals like *DZone*. He has been a member of the Java EE, EJB, and JMS expert groups over the years. Reza implemented the EJB container for the Resin open source Java EE application server. He helps lead the Philadelphia Java User Group. Reza is proud to be a founding member of the Jakarta EE Ambassadors.

Reza has over a decade of experience with technology leadership, enterprise architecture, and consulting. He has been working with Java EE technology since its inception, developing on almost every major application platform ranging from Tomcat to JBoss, GlassFish, WebSphere, and WebLogic. Reza has developed enterprise systems for well-known companies like eBay, Motorola, Comcast, Nokia, Prudential, Guardian Life, USAA, Independence Blue Cross, Anthem, Capital One, and AAA using Java EE and Spring. He is particularly interested in distributed systems, messaging, middleware, persistence, and machine learning.

Reza is an inductee to Phi Beta Kappa, the oldest and most respected national honor society for undergraduates in liberal arts and sciences. He earned his bachelor's degree from Gettysburg College. He graduated summa cum laude with a double major in computer science and economics as well as a minor in mathematics.

Foreword

From the streets of Cairo and the Arab Spring, to Occupy Wall Street, from the busy political calendar to the aftermath of the tsunami in Japan, social media was not only sharing the news but driving it.

—Dan Rather (American journalist, eight-time Peabody award winner)

Freedom of expression, especially when inspired by innocent intention, is the defining force behind open societies. This powerful force now has new wings thanks to social media. Social media grants voice to the unheard all around this ever turbulent little planet of ours, and we are still only beginning to see what it can do – be it in Kiev, Moscow, Minneapolis, Ferguson, Tunis, Cairo, Riyadh, Tehran, Hong Kong, Beijing, Tel Aviv, or Gaza.

Despite the pivotal role social media plays in modern life, there are few books that cover the topic of social media and Java. What little material there is usually covers the most common use case – federated security using OIDC and JWT. Perhaps consequently, there are few Java applications that fully utilize social media despite the wide open space of what is possible. This is precisely why this book is so important. It provides a great background of the social media industry, explains the core concepts important for Java social media developers, describes the so far relatively feeble efforts toward standardization, outlines social security for Java, and of course covers the social media frameworks and APIs most relevant to Java. Given the volatility, breadth, depth, and complexity of the topic, this book was no doubt a very tough one to write. To boot I can't think of a better person than Werner to write the book. He has been involved in the space for a long time ever since the Agorava project and the nascent effort to standardize a social media API in Java. His command of the space is evident throughout the book.

I hope the book will prove invaluable to any Java social media developer.

—Reza Rahman
Principal Program Manager, Java on Azure at Microsoft
Jakarta EE Ambassador, author, speaker

CHAPTER 1

Introduction

This chapter tells the history of social media from ancient days until more recently. The first few decades of the 21st century are often considered the "heydays" of social media between the "DotCom Bubble" and the financial crisis of 2008. We look further into the years that came after that, until the very recent history and what the future might bring for social media.

Ancient History

Most people assume social media to be a modern-day invention of companies like Facebook, Twitter, Google, Myspace, and Yahoo! In actual fact, social media has a history that reaches back over thousands of years.

To some, the postal service was one of the earliest forms of social media. From the days of the ancient Persian postal service to the Greek Agora [1] and Roman Forum [2], the postal service served as a medium for social and political discussion. The first recorded equivalents to Wiki or "Forum posts" were literally carved into the walls of Roman Forums or similar buildings [3], recording events like the destruction of Pompeii by Mount Vesuvius or several parts of Rome under Nero.

The Ancient Agora of Athens acted as an incubator to democracy being a favorite venue for social and political debate while doing business in ancient Greece. Until today, this worked in similar ways while the forums often turned digital. From Tunisia to Ukraine, opposition movements used social media to bring democracy to places where it's often been surprising and uncommon for a long time [4].

The telegraph was invented in 1792, allowing to deliver personal messages over long distances much faster than a horse rider or stagecoach could carry them. Although telegraph messages were short (much like SMS or tweets), they were a revolutionary way to spread news and exchange information. Many people think that was the birth of social media.

© Werner Keil 2024
W. Keil, *Enterprise Social for the Java Platform*, https://doi.org/10.1007/978-1-4842-9571-7_1

While several countries like the United States continue to offer postal telegrams, even to the President or other officials, the German postal service shut down its telegram service on New Year's Eve 2022 [39].

Figure 1-1. *Morse-Vail Telegraph Key*

Modern History

During the 20th century, information technology as we know it now started with pioneers like Konrad Zuse, George Stibitz, or Howard Aiken, and of course Alan Turing, who created the Turing test as a benchmark for AI and social bots.

Generation X

In 1975, shortly before the American military pulled out of Vietnam, the libertarian thinker Samuel Edward Konkin III introduced a philosophy called Agorism, a social philosophy of counter-economics and the ideas associated with that practice [5]. In a market anarchist society, law and security would be provided by market actors instead of political institutions. Agorists recognize that the situation cannot develop through political reform. Instead, it shall arise as a result of market processes. Aspects of its social values can be found today in the Occupy Movement, its primary goal being to make the economic and political relations in all societies less vertically hierarchical and more flatly distributed. Or in protest parties like Beppe Grillo in Italy, Syriza in Greece (where it even took over government), Podemos in Spain, or the Pirate Parties. Agorism also put forth the idea of using different currencies, something modern social media and related online communities are adopting with digital currencies like Bitcoin.

In 1966, the email was invented, ARPANET, a network of computers created by the US military about a year later, followed by the arrival of CompuServe in 1969. CompuServe launched its email service in the late 1980s and expanded into early 1990s, before finally dissolving original CompuServe in 2009 after several takeovers.

Usenet started up in 1979 and provided its users with forums and newsgroups. Surprisingly, most of their functions have changed very little and still exist today.

Internet Relay Chat (IRC) began in 1988 and was widely used across academic networks before emerging into what is now the Internet. IRC remains quite active today, although it is largely overshadowed by other short messaging services like Twitter. There are still around 3200 IRC servers around the world with hundreds of thousands of channels available.

Millennials

Based on the notion of Six Degrees of Separation [6], the first modern social network, sixdegrees.com, was founded in 1997. It allowed members to link to other members as friends, write messages, or post on bulletin boards. After being sold onto another company for $125 million, it was shut down in 2001 with roughly around one million users. It later made a minor comeback and still exists today.

When services like Amazon, Yahoo!, and, in 1998, Google first came into existence, they were not considered social networks. In 1995, Microsoft picked up on the emerging trends by launching the Microsoft Network (MSN). MSN became known as a "portal," another word for personalized online community. It wasn't surprising when many portal products, servers, and vendors jumped the social bandwagon a few years later.

Both Microsoft and Yahoo! had fallen behind some of social media's new kids on the block, and besides a rather brilliant and fast move with YouTube, most other aspects of social media were also a bit underestimated by Google, until it returned via Google+ and is certainly here to stay even if it may not lead every aspect of it. Yahoo! also offers plenty of social features and has since its recent recovery taken over smaller vendors in the social networking space like Flickr or Tumblr. In 1999, Brad Fitzpatrick, who later also worked at Google, founded LiveJournal.

Generation Z

At the start of the 2000s, many social networks were founded, although not so many of them survived until today. Hot or Not (AmIHotOrNot.com) was founded in October 2000 by James Hong and Jim Young, two friends and fellow students at the University of California in Berkeley. The initial motivation for the site was an argument about women's attractiveness by the founders. It was the first site to upload photos for others to rate and allegedly influenced the creators of Facebook or YouTube. In 2008, Hot or Not was sold for a rumored $20 million to the owners of online dating service Ashley Madison (which later became infamous for losing all its customer data to hackers) and in 2012 purchased by Badoo, which is now part of the Bumble dating app conglomerate.

While the URL still exists, the app has been rebranded to "Chat & Date" and has very little in common with the original site, but Hot or Not can of course be seen as the first predecessor to modern dating apps like Tinder.

Friendster, founded in 2002, was originally also planned as a dating site similar to Hot or Not, but it became a site to connect with like-minded people and their common friends. It contained a profile and status updates, allowing you to share your mood and exchange messages.

Until early 2004 it was the biggest and most popular social network, something that eventually doomed it, because it could not scale to handle user demand and left many of them frustrated, looking for alternatives. In 2003, Google offered $30 million to purchase Friendster, but the founders turned that offer down. In 2009, it was acquired after all by an Internet company named MOL Global in Kuala Lumpur. Besides a mostly Asian user base, Friendster's patents were also a vital asset, including one for a "system, method, and apparatus for connecting users in an online computer system based on their relationships within social networks." Most of these core social infrastructure patents were bought by Facebook for $40 million in 2010.

A year later Friendster became a social gaming site. On June 14, 2015, the site was shut down, and three years later in 2018, the company was terminated.

Also founded in 2002, LinkedIn, later sometimes considered a "Myspace for adults," was the first social network to offer users a paid premium package. Its job market and subscriptions helped it to become profitable in 2006. The job market and online resume would become a key feature, making it a more professional social network compared to others.

In 2011, LinkedIn filed an IPO. Five years later in 2016, Microsoft acquired LinkedIn for $26.2 billion, the second largest acquisition behind the video game producer

Activision Blizzard, Microsoft tried to buy for $68.7 billion in 2022 [42]. UK regulators had raised concerns, but eventually on October 13, 2023 (even a Friday) they approved it.

Myspace (MySpace before its rebranding in 2012), Friendster's biggest rival that started in 2003, benefited most from frustration about the technical issues. Originally inspired by Friendster, it also offered some improvements like customization or public profiles that did not require logging into it first. In February 2005, MySpace rejected an offer by Mark Zuckerberg to sell Facebook for $75 million. Just a few months later, Fox News parent company News Corporation purchased MySpace itself for USD 580 million. Until 2008 MySpace was the leading social networking site, but it was surpassed by Facebook in 2009 and since then rapidly lost users. In June 2011, Specific Media Group and Justin Timberlake purchased Myspace for approximately $35 million after News Corp had nearly paid a billion 6 years earlier. A reason for Timberlake's involvement was that Myspace had its own record label after the News Corp. takeover and it generally appealed more to artists. Between 2016 and 2018 through a series of takeovers, Myspace got purchased by what's now the Dotdash Meredith media group.

It still exists with roughly around six million users, compared to hundreds of millions during its heyday.

Also, in 2003, Mark Zuckerberg launched Facemash, a kind of Harvard University's answer to Berkeley's Hot or Not, rebranding it as "The Facebook" in 2004. The one millionth user joined the same year.

In 2005, the site dropped the "the" and became just "Facebook," after the "Facebook. com" domain was purchased for $200k, which seemed like a bargain compared to several takeovers, most notably Facebook buying up Instagram for close to a billion dollars or its gigantic takeover bid for the mobile messaging service WhatsApp.

Around that time a myriad of social networking sites came into existence. Photo sharing sites like Photobucket of Flickr, social bookmarking site del.icio.us, Reddit, or the blogging platform WordPress all started between 2003 and 2005.

StudiVZ and derivatives like SchülerVZ or MeinVZ were a social network for students, founded on November 11, 2005 (coincidentally both "Singles Day" and the beginning of Carnival) in Berlin by two students named Ehssan Dariani (who became CEO) and Dennis Bemmann. A major feature of StudiVZ was the so-called "gruscheln" (a mix of the German words "grüßen" = greet and "kuscheln," meaning to cuddle). It was similar to Facebook's poking function, allowing users to write short notifications, or the feature InterNations used to call "twinkle".

As of 2010, the VZ Networks claimed a total user base of over 16 million users. However, soon after, many users became inactive or left the network, which faced a decline of 70–80% compared to the years before. On September 7, 2017, the owner Poolworks declared StudiVZ bankrupt. In March 2022, the network was shut down.

YouTube also started in 2005, a year after competing the online video site Vimeo. The first video was "Me at the zoo" [40] filmed in the San Diego Zoo, which so far (Q1/2023) had over 260 million views since then. Just a year later in 2006, Google acquired YouTube for $1.65 billion.

2006 was also the year Twitter hatched. Similar to Facebook, the name changed slightly, but notably from "Twttr" to an easier to pronounce name. The first tweet was posted by co-founder Jack Dorsey (@Jack) on March 21, 2006: "just setting up my twttr."

A year later the hashtag was invented. The symbol was inspired by the channel names in IRC, now used by many leading social networks. Initially Twitter had a character limit of 140 characters, along the lines of SMS text messages. It took over a decade to double that to 280 in 2017.

In 2007, Twitch was launched, then under the name Justin.tv by Yale graduates Justin Kan and Emmett Shear. By 2013, the company had become profitable and had over 43 million monthly users. A year later, in 2014 after speculations about a YouTube acquisition, Amazon acquired Twitch Interactive for USD 970 million.

Here and Now

In recent years, the majority of developments in social media were either security breaches and other difficulties or mergers and acquisitions, with a few notable exceptions.

In 2015, Discord, an instant messaging and VoIP social platform, was founded. It soon became widely used by esports and LAN tournament gamers and benefited from relationships with Twitch streamers, as both platforms reach out to similar user groups, especially gamers.

In 2016, Mastodon, a free, decentral, and open source software to create social networking services based on open standards and protocols (commonly referred to as the "Fediverse"), was launched.

In 2017, ByteDance acquired Musical.ly for $1 billion while also launching short video sharing service TikTok. Far-Right microblogging site Gab also started in 2017, while AIM and Beme were shut down.

In 2018, Yahoo! Messenger was shut down, and Musical.ly got merged into TikTok. Another self-proclaimed "Free Speech" network, Parler, started the same year, also primarily used by right-wing and other extremists or conspiracy theorists, especially after the COVID-19 pandemic started in 2020. While he did not go through with it, Kanye West considered buying Parler after he was banned from nearly every other major site following antisemitic statements [46]. In April 2023, soon after they purchased Parler, the CEO of the new owner Starboard had it shut down, citing that "No Reasonable Person Believes Twitter For Conservatives Is A Viable Business Model" [52].

In 2019, Google+ was shut down, and Verizon sold Tumblr to Automattic, the owner of WordPress.com and key supporter of WordPress for less than $3 million [43].

2020 saw the launch of the audio-chat messaging app Clubhouse and BeReal, a social media app with a focus on authenticity. Especially in an era dominated by "Fake News," it gained popularity since then.

In 2021, both Gettr, another social media platform for unfiltered content mostly from Alt-Right users was founded by Jason Miller, a former aide to ex-President Donald Trump, and Trump himself started Truth Social, based on Mastodon, but without being open to the Fediverse [45]. After it had started as a Twitter project to create a decentralized social network protocol, in October 2021, Twitter co-founder and former CEO, Jack Dorsey as well as Jay Graber, who used to work for crypto company Zcash founded Bluesky Social. Graber has been the Bluesky CEO since then. While Bluesky had received funding from Twitter through Elon Musk's takeover, it raised $8 million in a seed funding round in July 2023, in order to be financially independent from Twitter under Musk. A few weeks earlier, in May 2023, Bluesky also made its social media client open source under the MIT license, after it had already published underlying protocols like the Authenticated Transfer Protocol (AT Protocol or atproto) the year before. Atproto is a federated protocol for building open social media applications. While not fully considered part of the Fediverse, there are efforts to create bridges between it and Bluesky. Given most of it is open source and shares goals with standards and protocols in the Fediverse, interoperability with Bluesky is likely going to happen sooner than later. An interesting feature of Bluesky is a multi-lingual approach. Posts can declare up to 3 languages. The list contains pretty much every known language, even Esperanto, Latin or Yiddish. Via "content languages" in account settings, users can select which languages they want to see in their social feed. Although some social networks like LinkedIn also offer i18n for profiles, the level of language support by Bluesky seems pretty unique. As of late September 2023, the number of Bluesky users exceeded 1.15 million. Still an invite-only beta phase, it should grow even faster, once it was opened to the general public. Especially if the former Twitter network under Elon Musk degrades further into a right-wing boys club, starts charging everyone even for basic use, or a combination of these factors.

In 2022, Yik Yak returned to Android, after it had already been available on iOS the year before. In the summer of 2022, Google's Lambda AI passed the Turing test, followed by ChatGPT toward the end of the same year [49]. And of course, the dominating event of the year, particularly for social media, was Elon Musk's $44 billion purchase of Twitter.

While Twitter had also blocked accounts earlier [50] soon after Elon Musk's takeover, a large number of accounts were blocked or suspended for sometimes dubious reasons, while others, mostly right-wing "conservatives," hate groups, anti-vaxxers, and similar conspiracy theorists, most notably Donald Trump himself, got their accounts reinstated. In an effort to mitigate the soaring losses of Twitter, a paid subscription replaced the prior verification of accounts. The vow to reduce bots and fake accounts also failed miserably, and now bots can even gain some sort of legitimacy by paying for the subscription, if those running them are willing to pay. While Musk reversed the ban on Trump's account, he openly supports Republican primary competitor DeSantis and even hosted a live event on Twitter announcing his campaign. However, that event became a disaster and humiliation for both, when almost nobody could attend the live stream and the video feed was practically nonexistent, leaving only their voice to be heard [53]. In late 2022, activists behind Occupy Democrats launched Tribel Social, a left-leaning, liberal social network with a motto of "morality, truth, and We the People first", adding to other Twitter alternatives. The site claims to have around half a million users.

In early June 2023, Reddit announced a steep increase in their API usage fees, hoping to boost chances of finally launching its long-announced IPO. According to the new pricing scheme, developers have to pay $12,000 per 50 million requests, driving many smaller or community-driven apps using Reddit out of business. This resulted in an attempted uprising by many moderators for parts of the network named "subreddits." Most of them were suspended by Reddit, although a few later got reinstated.

One argument besides trying to please investors was the rise of AI solutions like ChatGPT or Google's Lambda AI harvesting information sources like Reddit, Wikipedia, and others for their training, while these sites don't get rewarded for it. There was a great outrage when Twitter, in a desperate move to gather more money, said it would charge $42,000 for 50 million requests, which drove many smaller or community-driven sites like Unfollower Stats into shutting down as well. Despite Reddit's promise to avoid that kind of extreme pricing, their price is "still $12,000."

On July 5, 2023, Meta, the parent company to Facebook, Instagram, or WhatsApp, launched a new "microblogging" service named Threads in an apparent blow to Twitter [57]. A decentralized social network, developed by Instagram, it so far also requires an existing Instagram account. Due to EU privacy laws, Threads is not available in the EU until further notice.

In the first few days, it was possible to install and use Threads via mobile VPN, so I gave it a try, but Meta prevented that, leading to a decline in usage after an initial surge to over 100 million users. It seems Threads could soon be used in the EU and other countries without VPN.

On July 24, 2023, Elon Musk had Twitter's name changed to "X" [58]. Hoping to mimic some of what WeChat does in China, Musk seemingly ignores that what's possible in China with a different approach to privacy and the power concentration by a single company (as long as it plays by the rules of the political establishment) may not work in other countries, even the United States, let alone EU countries. The idea for "X" (oddly enough, Google/Alphabet also has a somewhat secret "Skunkworks" kind of lab named X) is not new, and Elon Musk already registered the domain back in his PayPal days; before the company became PayPal, it was already called "X.com", but he was ousted after a somewhat hostile takeover (note the irony) by X's biggest competitor Confinity with their product "PayPal" and replaced by Peter Thiel as CEO. A key reason was Musk being torn apart by many different ideas and goals for "X", while the others led by Thiel just wanted to focus on payments, which the company also succeeded until today.

Of course Musk is now much wealthier than Thiel and currently the richest man in the world, but it remains to be seen which of the many ideas for "X" he'll accomplish this time and which of these services (most will be paid and likely more than just 8$ per month) users accept to pay for, instead of using them elsewhere, including PayPal, Stripe, Amazon, and many others for online payments. Not to mention possible antitrust violations, if the app became too big or say, future buyers of a Tesla were forced to use the X payment system only, or by forcing everyone to watch SpaceX launches on X instead of YouTube despite a worse user experience and performance. Shortly after the name change, the "Twitter bird" was replaced by an "X" logo that bears the sentiment of the X Window System, and terms like "tweet" were replaced by "post", just like any other social network, losing even more of the unique brand recognition it once had. On September 18, 2023 Elon Musk announced that he might put X behind a paywall for all users, followed by a trial run of charging a so-far "symbolic" 1 $ in the Philippines and New Zealand. Although he claims to fight bots and fake accounts, it's the latest desperate measure to get some money out of the expensive toy. Many experts agree, it could be the final nail in the coffin of X/Twitter and its user base may sooner than later shrink to a level of MySpace or Truth Social.

Future

Social networks have always existed, since people first started to communicate. Technical means changed over time and are likely to change even faster in the near future. Some services will be merged; others might become irrelevant and vanish sooner or later. Using vendor-neutral standards and frameworks that won't tie you into the offerings of just a single provider is crucial, unless you want to spend more time on rapidly changing APIs than actually using it for something productive, or worse, having to switch over to another provider if proprietary API and framework offered by a particular vendor are no longer available. While not a social network in the sense of Twitter or Facebook, one of the first crypto trading bankruptcies of Mt. Gox [7], long before the likes of FTX, BlockFi, Celsius, or Voyager, was a good example for such a dilemma. It used to be a market leader in this area for some time. Therefore, applications and e-commerce solutions offering Bitcoin through its API were forced to rewrite or throw those apps away.

If a vendor-neutral abstraction is created on top of such API, then it is much easier to cope with problems and changes like those caused by a vendor going out of business, being taken over by others, or a combination of both, like it still keeps looming for Twitter/X since the Elon Musk takeover and subsequent rebranding.

This is where vendor- and social service-neutral approaches like the Fediverse, Agorava, Keycloak, or Jakarta EE come into play.

Summary

In this chapter, we learned about the history of social media, its boom years, what is happening right now, and where the future direction could lead to. As well as how mergers and acquisitions can sometimes pose a risk for your social media strategies, especially if some of the new owners are double-minded and eccentric to put it mildly.

CHAPTER 2

Social Use Cases

In this chapter, we are going to explore the various use cases for social media, from general purpose networks to technically specialized ones like media sharing, as well as vertical social networks catering to a certain target group.

Types of Social Networks

There are numerous social media websites either for general purpose or focus groups and specialized communities, including former alcoholics, music fans, developers, expats, mothers, students, teachers, government employees, and people who are into gardening, knitting, or BDSM. The "Fifty Shades of Grey" books and films probably added even more shades to that list [17].

Traditional Social Networks

Most people are familiar with traditional social networking sites like

- Facebook
- Twitter
- Mastodon
- Myspace
- WeChat
- Sina Weibo

These platforms help us connect with friends, family, fellow students, or people who share common interests.

© Werner Keil 2024
W. Keil, *Enterprise Social for the Java Platform*, https://doi.org/10.1007/978-1-4842-9571-7_2

Business and Enterprise

These are popular social networks for business:

- LinkedIn
- XING

These are mostly used for work or job seeking, as a digital CV. LinkedIn was purchased by Microsoft and is a global player. XING originated in Hamburg, Germany, and is therefore active mostly in Europe. It acquired several other job portals or hiring services, as well as InterNations, the biggest social network for expats, adding users in 420 global communities anywhere from Honolulu to Auckland.

Messaging Services

These are the most popular social messaging services:

- WhatsApp
- Facebook Messenger
- Telegram
- Discord
- Viber
- WeChat
- Snapchat
- Line
- QQ
- Signal
- KakaoTalk
- Zalo

Media Sharing

Media sharing sites fall into three categories:

1. Audio sharing

2. Image sharing

3. Video sharing

Audio Sharing

Audio sharing can be

- Music sharing/streaming

- Podcasts

- Audiobooks

Music Sharing/Streaming

There are several music sharing and streaming portals. One of the earliest, founded in 1996, which still exists, is the Live Music Archive (LMA). It provides over 250,000 live concert recordings of mostly indie artists but also some big names like the Grateful Dead.

Also, around the turn of the century came Napster, founded by Sean Parker, who later came to fame and fortune with Facebook. It was mostly decentral and free but in its original form had been forced to shut down due to copyright infringement. However, its third iteration still exists today.

While Apple Music started only in 2015, its roots go back to Apple iTunes, in existence since 2001.

Many music sharing sites were started in the prolific years for social media between 2001 and 2010, among them:

- Myspace

- DatPiff

- Jamendo

- Mixcloud

- Musopen

- Spotify

- SoundCloud

- Deezer

- Noise Trade

- Playlist

- StarMaker

- Smule

Besides Apple, Internet and social media giants Amazon and Google also provide music downloads and streaming, sometimes through various brands like Google Play Music and YouTube Music.

Podcasts

The Podcast was invented by Tristan Louis and Dave Winer in 2000, based on the RSS format. Initially called "Audioblogging," British digital journalist Ben Hammersley coined the term "podcast" in an article for *The Guardian* from 2004. The inspiration was Apple's iPod music player.

Obviously, Apple was among the first to offer podcasts on iTunes. Nowadays besides radio and TV stations, all major players in music and streaming also provide podcasts.

Audiobooks

There is a thin line between podcasts and audiobooks; both are often hosted by the same channels. First invented by Thomas Edison through his phonograph, audiobooks originally targeted mostly blind people, allowing them to listen to stories instead of reading them.

Audiobooks evolved with recording devices from audio cylinders for almost 100 years to acetate and vinyl discs, compact cassettes, minidisks, CDs, or DVDs and ultimately solid-state storage like the iPod or server racks of a streaming server.

Besides book publishing houses and radio or TV stations, audiobooks are offered by most major Internet giants and providers of podcasts or music streaming services.

Image Sharing

As we learned, the first social network to upload pictures was Hot or Not in 2000. The first camera phone was created three years earlier by former Borland founder Philippe Kahn, with almost MacGyver improvised installations, to share the birth of his daughter in real time with selected friends [47].

These are some of the top image sharing apps:

- Adobe Creative Cloud – For Photoshop users

- Google Photos – Photo storage and backup

- iCloud Drive – Photo storage backup for Apple users

- Instagram – Instant messaging and photo sharing

- Pinterest – Visually share ideas like recipes, home decoration, or other information

- SmugMug – Secure your photos

- Amazon Photos – For Amazon Prime customers

- Waldo – Pro-level options for photography corporations

- The Guest – Automatic photo uploader

- Internxt Photos – Exceptionally fast photo exchange

- Imgur – Content hosting site where you can view and share images, GIFs, memes, or videos

- FamilyAlbum – For family photos

- Flickr – Community of photographers

- Snapchat – Multimedia instant messaging

- Pixpa – Easily sell photos

- 500px – Sharing and communication

Besides those dedicated photo apps, nearly every major social networking site like Facebook or Twitter also allows sharing and storing images, although the level of convenience is not always a match to specialized photo services.

Video Sharing

YouTube revolutionized the way we watch and create videos. It could turn almost everyone with a mobile device into a director of photography and helped create a special kind of influencers: YouTubers, many of them earning money comparable to movie stars.

These are 11 important video sharing sites:

- YouTube
- Vimeo
- TikTok
- Dailymotion
- Metacafe
- Instagram IGTV
- Facebook Watch
- Kuaishou
- Periscope
- Utreon
- TED

Video Streaming

These are ten important video streaming sites:

- Amazon Prime
- Apple TV+
- discovery+
- Disney+
- Google Play Video
- Netflix
- Paramount+

- Twitch

- YouTube

- WOW

Many are video streaming channels, where studios rather than users themselves publish the content.

Even those mostly offer some degree of social interaction, from simple like (or dislike) buttons to reviews or even social gatherings like Amazon Watch Parties or the Disney+ GroupWatch feature.

Others, especially YouTube or Twitch, are social streaming sites where members of the community share live streams, often computer gaming, esports, education, concerts, or similar live events. Both "YouTubers" and Twitch "Streamers" can sometimes reach fame and fortune, if their content attracts millions of followers, which also leads to six- or seven-digit annual income for some of the top content creators.

Blogging and Writing

These are the best social media platforms for bloggers and writers:

- Tumblr

- Facebook

- Pinterest

- Medium

- Instagram

- Goodreads

Discussion Forums

While there can be heated discussions on Twitter (even more, after Elon Musk took it over and opened the floodgates to right-wing conspiracy theories) or Facebook, discussion sites like Reddit and Quora are specifically designed to spark a conversation.

These are popular social media discussion forums:

- Reddit

- Facebook

- Quora

- LinkedIn

- Stack Overflow

- Digital Point

- Webmaster Sun

Review Sites

The top ten review sites are shown in Table 2-1.

Table 2-1. *Best Review Sites*

Site	Category	Avg. Monthly US Traffic	% US Traffic (Total)
Google Business Profile	Any business	158.03 million	19.6%
Amazon	E-commerce	85.44 million	63.6%
Facebook	Any business	85.57 million	23.1%
Yelp	Any business	40.47 million	87,5%
Tripadvisor	Food, restaurant, travel	28.27 million	50.4%
BBB (Better Business Bureau)	Any business	6.15 million	72.1%
Yellow Pages	Any business	10.5 million	70.0%
Manta	Any business	6.48 million	67.0%
Angi	Services	5.44 million	72.4%
Foursquare	Mostly shops and restaurants	3.67 million	19.3%

VR/Metaverse

Facebook changed its name to Meta in a bet on the Metaverse that has to fully manifest. Besides Meta, Apple, which often managed to disrupt established markets with products like the iPod, iPhone, or Apple Watch, also threw its Vision Pro headset into the ring.

These are the top social VR apps:

- AltspaceVR
- BeanVR
- Bigscreen
- Couch
- Horizon Venues
- Horizon Worlds
- Rec Room
- Sansar
- Second Life
- Sensorium Galaxy
- VRChat
- VRzone
- vTime XR

Vertical Social Networks

Vertical social networks are specialized social media platforms dedicated to the interests of particular communities, like developers, gamers, investors, neighbors, and garden or book lovers.

Development

These are the top five social developer platforms:

- GitHub
- GitLab

- Bitbucket
- Launchpad
- SourceForge

Finance

There are several social networks for finance and investment, including the following:

- eToro – A social trading and investment platform that allows users to trade and invest in various financial instruments, such as stocks, currencies, and commodities. It also allows users to follow and copy the trades of other successful investors on the platform.

- Stocktwits – A social network for investors and traders to share and discuss market insights, news, and analysis. It is a community-driven platform that allows users to share their thoughts on individual stocks and other financial instruments in real time.

- Seeking Alpha – A social media platform for investors and traders, providing real-time financial news, analysis, and research on stocks and other investments. It also allows users to share their insights and opinions with the community.

These social networks can be valuable resources for investors and traders to stay up to date with the latest news, analysis, and insights on the financial markets, as well as to connect and engage with other like-minded professionals or hobby investors.

Health and Fitness

There are many social networks and portals dedicated to health and fitness. While many fitness, health, or nutrition influencers just use Facebook, Twitter, or Instagram to flash their abs, an increasing number of people use wearables and similar smart devices to quantify various health conditions, ranging from sleep patterns, to body weight, to heart rates. Of these "Quantified Selves," many choose to openly share their data through social networks.

Many smartwatch makers have their own proprietary apps, but there are also fitness and smart device portals by platform providers like

- Apple Health
- Google Fit

- Fitbit (now also Google)

- Strava

- Adidas (Runtastic)

- MyFitnessPal

Apple Health

Apple Health is primarily a mobile app for iOS and a companion for Apple Watch. The app adds trend analysis for 20 types of data, from resting heart rate to sleep or cardio fitness, allowing users to see how a given metric is progressing.

With their permission, so far mostly in the United States, users can also share selected health information with their doctor or insurance company.

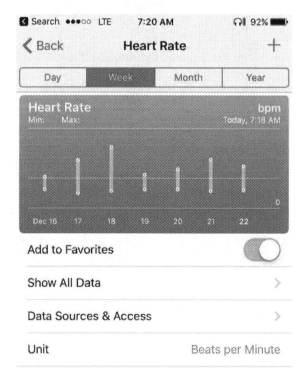

Figure 2-1. *Apple Health: Heart Rate*

Since watchOS 5, there's a new Apple Watch activity feature to motivate people to work out and compete with their friends. They can challenge any friend to a seven-day competition from their Apple Watch, who can fill out their activity rings faster, see Figure 2-2.

Figure 2-2. *Apple Health: Competitions*

Google Fit

Google Fit is a health-tracking platform by Google for the Android operating system. It allows users to monitor and track various types of health and fitness information, such as activity level, heart rate, weight, steps walked, or sleep.

Google Fit aggregates data from multiple sensor devices and third-party apps, making it easy for users to view and manage their health and fitness data in one place.

Figure 2-3. *Google Fit Dashboard*

Users can set and track goals, such as a daily step count, weight loss, hours of sleep, or a weekly running goal, and receive personalized insights and recommendations based on their activity. Google Fit aims to help users improve their health and wellness by making it easier to manage their fitness goals and monitor their progress over time, but Google Fit so far offers no sharing or competing with others; unlike Apple, Adidas, or Strava, there are no challenges at this point in Google Fit. In 2019, the Google Fit web app was discontinued.

Fitbit

Fitbit was purchased by Google in 2019. While a tighter integration with a Google account, especially for new users and newly registered devices, is underway, the brand is still somewhat independent, although it could be seen as an equivalent to other Google brands like "Pixel."

Until 2025 Google promised the old legacy accounts would still run without a Google Account; after that, it becomes mandatory, or maybe the Fitbit app and dashboard (see Figure 2-4) may even be merged into Google Fit.

Figure 2-4. *Fitbit Dashboard*

Fitbit offers tracking of nutrition and exercises, as well as a form of gamification via badges or challenges, but under Google, most likely to cut costs, those features were scrapped in late March 2023 [51]. Fitbit users are not happy with that move. Fitbit had 31 million active users in 2020, an increase of 4% on the previous year (before the Google takeover). However, the global market share – Fitbit once accounted for 45% in 2014 – went below 3% in 2020. And while Apple has been the leading smartwatch brand for some time now with close to 30% market share, Google was still second with 8% at the end of 2022, but for all brands combined, with the Pixel watch likely ahead of its Fitbit devices.

Strava

Strava is a fitness portal with strong social characteristics. The majority of users may focus on running or cycling, but it offers dozens of different sports including yoga or snowshoe walking.

Unlike most other fitness portals with an emphasis on casual or semiprofessional athletes, there are also professional athletes like professional cyclists using it.

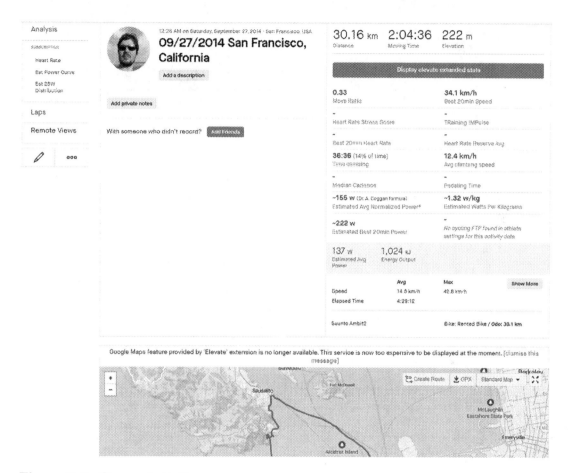

Figure 2-5. *Strava Activity*

Features include clubs and routes to share with others, as well as challenges for other users to compete with each other and integration with numerous devices like cyclometers or fitness trackers and smartwatches.

JavaOne Geek Bike Riders Edit Club

🚲 ▓ San Francisco, California

The Silicon Valley JUG will host the annual Geek Bike Ride the Saturday before JavaOne. We'll meet at Pier 41 in Fisherman's Wharf and ride across the bridge and down into Sausalito, and then take a ferry back to the city.

Figure 2-6. *Strava Club*

Some features require a paid subscription, but there are still enough that can be used without paid membership.

Adidas/Runtastic

The initial idea came up during a project at the University of Applied Sciences Upper Austria in 2006 to track sailboats, leading to Runtastic, founded in 2009.

In August 2015, it was announced that Adidas had acquired Runtastic for €220 million ($240 million), including a 50.1% stake, newspaper group Axel Springer held since 2013.

MyFitnessPal

MyFitnessPal is a smartphone and web application, allowing users to track their calorie intake, exercise, and other fitness information. It is a digital food diary that helps people monitor their daily food consumption to achieve their health and fitness goals.

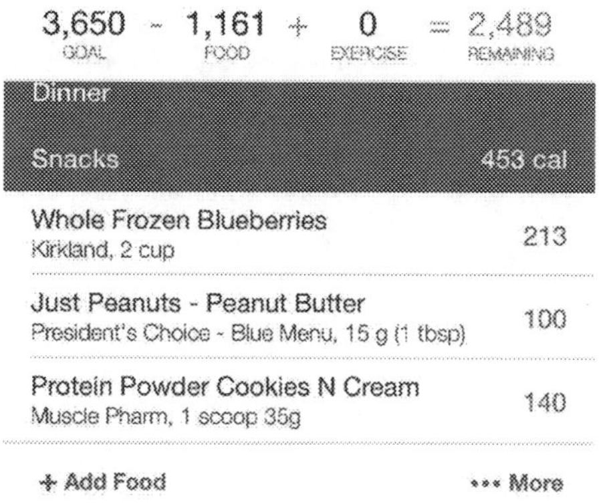

Figure 2-7. *MyFitnessPal*

The app has a database of over seven million foods, allowing users to log their meals, or scan barcodes on the packages for easy tracking. It also includes features to track liquid intake and consumed carbohydrates, protein, or fat, as well as exercises, which can be synced with other fitness apps and wearable devices like smartwatches or scales.

In February 2015, the sportswear company Under Armour acquired MyFitnessPal, but in 2020, it sold it again to a private equity firm. Seemingly to cut costs under the new management, in 2022, even before Fitbit, MyFitnessPal removed most social features like challenges, leaving only a social share of nutrition or exercise.

Travel

Table 2-2 shows the top 20 social travel services. Their categories range anywhere from booking or accommodation to flying or social rides.

Table 2-2. *Top Travel Sites*

Site	Category	Region
Airbnb	Social Accommodation	Global
Google Travel	Travel Search and Content Syndication	Global
Travello	Social Travel	Global
TripIt	Social Travel	Global
Tripadvisor	Social Travel and Rating	Global

(continued)

Table 2-2. (*continued*)

Site	Category	Region
Travel Buddy	Social Travel	Global
FlyerTalk	Frequent Flyer Network	Global
Ever Travel	Social Travel	Eastern Europe
Backpackr	Backpacking Travel Community	Global
Trippy	Social Travel	Global
Uber	Ride Hailing	Global
Lyft	Ride Hailing	Global
Bolt	Ride Hailing	Global
DiDi	Ride Hailing	China
Share Now	Ride Sharing	Europe
Turo	Ride Sharing	America
Free Now	Ride Hailing	Europe
Ola	Ride Hailing	India, Commonwealth
Zipcar	Ride Sharing	Global

Mobile Usage

Mobile usage is not necessarily a type of social media, but more a different situation or environment for social media apps, although some apps, for example, Google Fit, are only available for mobile usage now.

Andreas M. Kaplan [41] grouped mobile social media applications into four main types:

1. Space-timers – Location and time-sensitive: Sharing information is usually relevant to a particular location at a specific point in time. Examples are

    a. Foursquare Swarm

    b. Facebook Places

    c. WhatsApp

    d. Telegram

2. Space-locators – Location-sensitive only: Sharing information with relevance for a particular location, rating or tagging a place, which can later be read by others. Examples include

    a. Foursquare

    b. Yelp

    c. Fishbrain

    d. Qype

    e. Tumblr

3. Quick-timers – Time-sensitive only: The use of traditional social media on mobile apps to increase availability or as a second or third screen besides a TV screen, for example, watching your favorite show while tweeting about it. Includes

    a. Twitter

    b. Facebook

    c. Mastodon

4. Slow-timers – Neither time nor location-sensitive: The use of traditional social media on mobile apps, for example, watching a video on YouTube and reading/writing a Wikipedia article or Tumblr blog.

Summary

In the first two chapters, you've been introduced to the historical background of social media, followed by various use cases anywhere from following your friends and relatives online to professional usage by influencers and others using enterprise social for a living.

CHAPTER 3

Standardization

This chapter explores the efforts to standardize access to social media via common APIs, as well as some standards used by social networks themselves, allowing not only to switch more easily between different networks but also analyze data across different sources and social networks.

Types of Standards

Aside from their lobbying of "Basic Standards" like OpenSocial [15], Figure 3-1 provides an overview of social standards by Dachis Group from a series of articles [16].

Figure 3-1. *What's missing in Social Business Standards?*

© Werner Keil 2024
W. Keil, *Enterprise Social for the Java Platform*, https://doi.org/10.1007/978-1-4842-9571-7_3

Two main categories are as follows:

1. Higher-order standards – Behavior and domain-driven business-oriented standards and APIs. Most of them not so clearly fleshed out by the authors of [16]

2. Basic standards – Some were mentioned before, here grouped into four subcategories:

    a. Contacts

    b. Activity/Messaging

    c. Integration/Interoperability

    d. Security

Then you may look at the way social standards, frameworks, and libraries communicate, by either

- Consuming information

- Analyzing information

- Transforming information

- Providing information

A typical example for consuming information would be showing your status in your favorite social networks inside another application, for example, your blog or corporate website.

Another one is if you include a map service to show directions to an event you host or participate in.

Analyzing information involves some sort of calculation, ranking or benchmarking. Often consuming more than one source of in-formation, so you can get a better picture. An example of such a service would be Klout. Where activities across multiple social networks influence your overall ranking.

Transforming information can be done either by merging and combining several data streams, a simple sum of two numbers, or if, for example, your travel booking site predicts the cost of a trip in your local currency based on conversion rates. Translation services like Google Translate would be another, more sophisticated example of transforming information.

Last but not least, providing information is any service or sometimes just content your application makes available to others, ideally via an API allowing others to consume, analyze, or transform it based on their needs.

Another way of looking at enterprise social networks, related standards, or products can be the following:

- Stand-alone products or services with social aspects that can be installed and used on their own. While some, for example, those embracing OpenSocial, aim to be interoperable with others, ideally across multiple vendors.

- Embedded social facets or features within a larger product or suite. A classic example would be Oracle Fusion Middleware, containing social functionality in the footsteps of BEA AquaLogic [13] or several other Oracle acquisitions [23] in the social sector since then.

- Speciality, often domain-specific or vertical social networks, for example, for healthcare, fashion, developers, pet owners, or any other area of interest to a significant community. You'll remember a range of these from the previous chapter.

OPENi [31], a social media research group funded by the European Union, tried to group social standards and APIs in a somewhat context-related manner:

- Activity API refers to a social, health, and behavioral activity log as reflected in multiple cloud-based services ranging from Social, Photo, and Video Sharing to Health and Location-Based Services. In essence, it includes all the social and personal activities of a user and is related with the logging activity of a device. Relevant categories: Gaming, Health, Location-Based Services, Music, Photo, Shopping, Social, Video.

- Advertising and analytics API enabling the collection, aggregation, and analysis of end user/customer's needs, interests, and preferences based onTheir interaction with advertising/marketing content.

- Application behavioral data.

- Social network interactions toward enabling personalized advertising services with enhanced end user added value. Relevant categories: Analytics, advertising.

- Location API enabling location awareness through Check-ins, Direction, Events, Reviews, and Tips. It is a strong contextual API with location, which can be extracted by a GPS sensor and can be mapped on a map. Relevant categories: Mapping, Location-Based Services, Social, Music.

- Media API bringing together photo, music, and video sharing services with file transfer and syncing functionalities. It is related to the Gallery Application and the file system of a device. Relevant categories: File Transfer and Syncing, Location-Based Services, Music, News, Photo, Social, Video.

- Products and services API embracing payments and shopping services. This special case of commercialization-relevant objects requires a strong API with transactional capabilities and enhanced security. It is related to the store application of a phone. Relevant categories: Location-Based Services, Payments, Shopping.

- Profiles API extrapolating information about people based on Analytics, Advertising, Contacts, Gaming, Health, Location-Based Services, Messaging and Chat, Music, Social, etc. Typically, people can be represented in various ways, with multiple profiles. This API brings all that information together: avatars, profiles, contacts, and accounts, interrelating different profiles, in different services. It is directly related to the Agenda application of a smartphone. Some relevant categories: Analytics, Advertising, Contacts, Gaming, Health, Location-Based Services, Messaging and Chat, Music, Film, etc.

- Search API, in order to find and retrieve information from the cloud-based services. It brings together existing search engines with distributed search functionalities among various platforms and is related to the search functionality found in a desktop or phone OS.

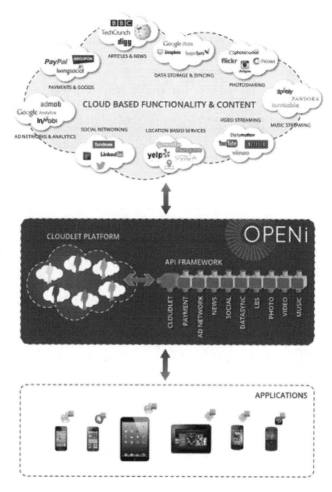

Figure 3-2. *OPENi concept*

While OPENi has not made any of their API available on GitHub (as their site promised in 2013), its work caught the attention of, for example, W3C where OpenSocial [15] is now further discussed. So even without APIs of its own, OPENi and its concepts may help there. We'll highlight OpenSocial in more detail when looking at Apache Shindig.

Apart from dissecting and categorizing social media standards as before, there are other standards and protocols many APIs and social networks use:

- Practically all social media services use **REST** as transmission protocol; some may use **SOAP**, but that's rather uncommon.

- Most of them transmit data in **JSON** format, some in **XML** or both.

- Identification and authentication are almost always based on **OAuth 2** or **OpenID Connect**.

Other basic standards and protocols not mentioned in Figure 3-1 as the list does not aim for completion are as follows:

- Open Graph Protocol (OGP) enables any web page to become a rich object in a social graph.

- oEmbed, a format allowing an embedded representation of a URL on third-party sites.

- PubSubHubbub, a simple, open, web-hook-based server-to-server pub-sub protocol.

- Salmon, a standard protocol for comments and annotations to swim upstream (hence the name) to original update sources.

We'll take a closer look at security aspects like authorization, authentication, or digital identity, as well as privacy, data protection, and related standards, in the next chapter.

Early Approaches

The theories that we encountered in the introduction, such as Six Degrees of Separation [6], influenced later concepts like Friend of a Friend (FOAF) [8]. Aspects of both can be found in most "Friend" mechanisms used by social networks today.

Rich Site Summary (RSS) [9] is an early example of a digital form of social media. Among the developers involved in the design and standardization of RSS was Reddit co-founder Aaron Swartz, who, before his untimely death in early 2013, had worked on a book about a Programmable Web [10], a rather down-to-earth, street-smart counterpart to the typically dry academic papers one finds in this field.

Portable Contacts was created by Plaxo, a social address book service founded in 2002 by a group of entrepreneurs around Sean Parker. Parker had legal troubles one wouldn't call so different from Aaron Swartz after his Napster music exchange portal was forced out of business, but fortunately talking for more than just one social media household name of today, he coped with it differently. The idea of a portable address book or set of "Digital Business Cards" was well intended and makes sense especially from a user's point of view, but commercial interests of competing players, each of them greedy to share data even with those who own it, created many roadblocks to an otherwise good idea. Plaxo while still in business after all those years was not necessarily his greatest hit, and investors kicked him out in ways not so different from what had happened to co-founder Eduardo Saverin at Facebook when Parker got involved. Financially this made him rich and put muscle behind other services, for example, Spotify. Little coincidence, it seems quite a bit like Napster, but in a more commercially accepted way, also thanks to his fame and fortune after Facebook. Portable Contacts may have been a significant part of the social media movement but is no longer used. This is because many of the APIs used within larger companies are no longer compatible with Portable Contacts. The only remainder still in use is vCard, used by many companies and applications.

Mashup

As the Java language played a more and more important role first on the desktop (mostly via Java applets in the early days, or AWT/Swing stand-alone applications) then around the turn of the century also on the server, Sun and other companies began to standardize parts of the Java platform in the Java Community Process (founded in 1998) or JCP [11]. Of the earliest members, IBM, Intel, Fujitsu, Sun, and Oracle (these two combined since 2010) are still active.

After being turned down or withdrawn twice, a notable standard for social networks, then often called "Portal" (see MSN earlier), was JSR 168, the Java Portlet Specification [48]. In an ideal world, it allowed portal applications to be deployed into multiple portal servers regardless of the vendor and together with other standards, especially the OASIS-defined WSRP (Web Services for Remote Portlets), raised hopes for interoperability between these applications even across different portals. After ten years, with other technologies and languages, especially "lightweight containers" on the rise, the Java Portlet standard got a version 3.0 update (JSR 362) in 2017, also planning to incorporate some social standards where possible but those did not make it into the Portlet spec anymore.

While Portlets and related standards are still mostly the domain of large-scale Enterprise Application servers inspired by music or video compilations or remixes, a more language and platform-neutral approach called Mashup [12] started shortly after the first Portlet standard. Whether it was Yahoo Pipes, Microsoft Popfly, Google Mashup Editor, IBM Mashup Center, or BEA AquaLogic [13], all of them promised interoperability and personalized widgets, with an experience similar to iGoogle. A service, mostly due to Google+ taking personalization and a more "Integrated Social Media" approach to the next level, was shut down on November 1, 2013.

So was RSS, only a few months after Aaron Swartz' death. Google Reader was discontinued on July 1, 2013. While Swartz as last documented in his unfinished book [10] advocated an open API-based programmable web, most of the big providers have different plans, as numerous articles around Google Reader's end like this one [14] express.

OStatus

OStatus is an open standard for federated microblogging, allowing users to receive status updates by users of another site. The standard combines a series of open protocols like

- Atom

- Activity Streams

- WebSub

- Salmon

- WebFinger

It started in 2013 with StatusNet, which later became GNU social [60]. It was at the time adopted by a number of microblogging sites, but frustration with the underlying technology turned most of them to use ActivityPub, including Mastodon [61], Pleroma, or postActiv. The only open source social network still using OStatus is Friendica [62], a very early open source approach that started in 2010 and is also written in PHP, like GNU social; hence, there seem to be more synergies between the two projects than for others.

OpenSocial

Another social standard has been shaped by community development almost since its inception: OpenSocial [15] developed by Google with a handful of initial supporters, MySpace still the most popular social network at the time, Ning or Plaxo. At this time Portable Contacts mentioned earlier would also fit into the overall idea of easy-to-use widgets and services across a variety of social networking providers, as opposed to, for example, version 2.0 of the Java Portlet standard, which released its Public Draft around the same time.

Seemingly easier to use, that also applied to exploits and security issues, often demonstrated by "script kiddies" more or less out of primary school using a few scripts to break or compromise those services and widgets. Full-scale Java EE servers and Portlets were and still are much harder to break into, if system administrators do their homework. And all the fuss about Java security or it being used to transport malware usually affects the client side.

A vast majority of OpenSocial is JavaScript code, making it more exposed than a mostly server-side or carefully mixed use of server (Jakarta EE or other environments) and client tier (JavaScript, etc.). See Figure 3-3 for different tiers of a typical web-based enterprise application using Java EE, but you may replace it by other languages like Python, PHP, Ruby, or Scala with the layers being about the same.

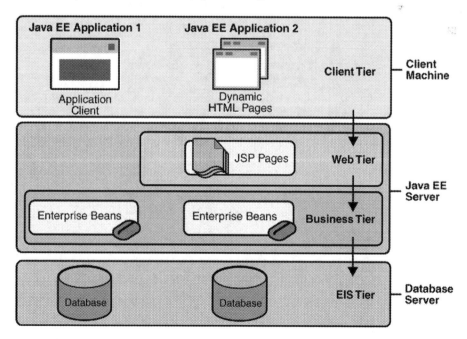

Figure 3-3. *N-tier Enterprise Application*

While Google began to use OpenSocial in its Orkut service (popular in Latin America and a few other countries like India, but never really picked up in other places), other vendors initially planning to support it abandoned those plans one after the other. The likes of LinkedIn or XING especially did so for security reasons. We'll hear more on security and privacy in the following chapter. Neither Facebook nor Twitter, the two dominating providers from the second half of the last decade, ever cared about OpenSocial. And more importantly, Google killed its own creation when it became obvious. Google+ would never support it either. A few vendors mainly from the server and large enterprise fraction like IBM, SAP, or Confluence author Atlassian still backed OpenSocial.

Dachis Group, in 2014 acquired by Sprinklr, sort of a "Think Tank" for social media and enterprise data analysis, was also strongly involved, though its focus goes more in directions like Big Data and NoSQL systems lately, and it openly admits like most remaining OpenSocial backers (or Thoughtworks in its regular survey called "Radar" about technologies to watch or regard less over time) the only place for it may be the enterprise and intranet after all. Big Data can be seen as a Mashup, too, but it takes place primarily on the EIS or DB tier (see Figure 3-4) so I won't discuss it much here. These technologies would also deserve their own book and exceed the scope of this one.

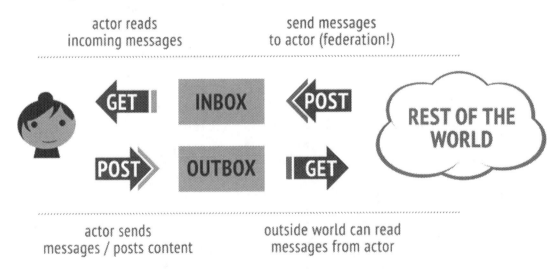

Figure 3-4. *ActivityPub Overview*

Instead of a seamless Mashup of, for example Google, Facebook, Twitter, LinkedIn, Microsoft, or Yahoo!, the only value of OpenSocial was connecting HR, Sales, or Accounting with each other and providing the management with some nifty "Social" Mashup of all departments and subsidiaries of a large enterprise, making it practically useless to those who wish to see, let's say, information from their Twitter feed next to the Facebook timeline. The purpose, OpenSocial was originally created for.

A twist in the OpenSocial story was an effort to create a W3C standard based on OpenSocial and similar concepts. What has been a hard and thorny path in the case of the Semantic Web seems almost impossible here, especially given a majority of players prefer their "walled garden" as we found earlier [14].

While W3C defined an interesting standard called semantic web, which sounds synergetic to some of OpenSocial's ideas, semantic web is so far used only in a few isolated sectors like biology or healthcare.

Work at W3C often happens at a rather slow pace, similar to (or even slower than) HTML5, for example, which, starting in 2008, was in candidate state (despite many vendors already proposing solutions and products being based on it) for some time. A final recommendation was published in late 2014, shortly after the W3C Social Web Working Group [30] started, remaining active till 2018, which, compared to most other W3C standards and working groups, was a fairly short duration.

W3C Social Web Protocols

The outcome of the W3C Social Web Working Group was a set of Social Web Protocols [63], allowing users of social networks to

- Create, update, and delete social content

- Connect with others by subscribing to their content

- Interact with other people's content

- Be notified when others interact with their content

Specifications

These are the specifications produced by the W3C Social Web Working Group:

- ActivityPub – JSON-LD-based APIs for client-to-server interactions like publishing and server-to-server interactions like federation

- ActivityStreams – The syntax and vocabulary to represent

  - Activity

  - Actor

- Link

- Object

- Collection

- Linked Data Notifications (LDN) – A JSON-LD-based protocol for delivery

- Micropub – A form-encoding and JSON-based API for client-to-server interactions like publishing

- Webmention – A form-encoding-based protocol for delivery

- WebSub – A protocol for subscriptions and delivery of updates to them

ActivityPub

ActivityPub is a decentralized social networking protocol based on the ActivityStreams 2.0 data format and JSON-LD.

It provides a client-to-server API for creating, updating, and deleting content and a federated server-to-server API to deliver notifications and subscribe to content.

In ActivityPub, users are called actors. Every actor has

- An **inbox** – To get messages by others

- An **outbox** – To send messages to others

Here's an example for the record of actor Alyssa:

```
{"@context": "https://www.w3.org/ns/activitystreams",
 "type": "Person",
 "id": "https://social.example/alyssa/",
 "name": "Alyssa P. Hacker",
 "preferredUsername": "alyssa",
 "summary": "Lisp enthusiast hailing from MIT",
 "inbox": "https://social.example/alyssa/inbox/",
 "outbox": "https://social.example/alyssa/outbox/",
 "followers": "https://social.example/alyssa/followers/",
 "following": "https://social.example/alyssa/following/",
 "liked": "https://social.example/alyssa/liked/"}
```

Imagine Alyssa wants to catch up with her friend, Ben. She lent him a book recently, and she wants to make sure he returns it. Here's the example message as an ActivityStreams object:

```
{"@context": "https://www.w3.org/ns/activitystreams",
 "type": "Note",
 "to": ["https://chatty.example/ben/"],
 "attributedTo": "https://social.example/alyssa/",
 "content": "Say, did you finish reading that book I lent you?"}
```

The server recognizes this is an object newly created and wraps it into a Create activity:

```
{"@context": "https://www.w3.org/ns/activitystreams",
 "type": "Create",
 "id": "https://social.example/alyssa/posts/a29a6843-9feb-4c74-
        a7f7-081b9c9201d3",
 "to": ["https://chatty.example/ben/"],
 "actor": "https://social.example/alyssa/",
 "object": {"type": "Note",
            "id": "https://social.example/alyssa/posts/49e2d03d-b53a-4c4c-
            a95c-94a6abf45a19",
            "attributedTo": "https://social.example/alyssa/",
            "to": ["https://chatty.example/ben/"],
            "content": "Say, did you finish reading that book I
            lent you?"}}
```

Alyssa's server looks up Ben's ActivityStreams actor object, finds his inbox endpoint, and POSTs her object to his inbox.

Adoption

After Mastodon already supported ActivityPub soon after it was finalized, several others followed, including Reddit, Goodreads, YouTube, or Tumblr; Flickr considers adding support as well. And Twitter/X rival Threads reportedly uses it or plans to add support soon [64].

Fediverse

The Fediverse (composed of "federation" and "universe") is a "global social network," allowing users of one service to communicate with users of other services using open protocols like ActivityPub. Notable social networks in the Fediverse are

- Mastodon

- Diaspora

- Friendica

- GNU social

- Hubzilla

- Lemmy

- PeerTube

- Pleroma

- Pixelfed

Many in the industry consider Elon Musk's Twitter takeover and transformation into his "X App" a huge catalyst for open social networks and the Fediverse. A statistics website called The-Federation.info, operated by Jason Robinson, lists the total users of the Fediverse as nearly 631 million, with roughly 7 million of them active over the last six months. Their statistics are voluntary and said to be incomplete; for example, Threads/Meta and several other large commercial players using standards and protocols from the Fediverse do not contribute to those stats; thus, the numbers may well be over a billion and active users probably in the tens of millions right now.

Other sites like Donald Trump's Truth Social [45] are based on open standards and pretty much a Mastodon rip-off, but they don't even interact with other sites through the Fediverse, nor contribute user stats in a transparent manner. The currently active users on Truth Social are said to be around half a million, compared to nearly two million active Mastodon users as of August 2023.

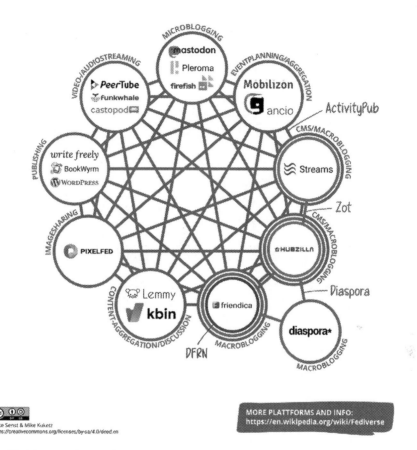

Figure 3-5. *Fediverse Overview*

Protocols

The-Federation.info currently lists 15 protocols used in the Fediverse:

- ActivityPub

- Bluesky

- DFRN

- Diaspora

- Gemini

- Inbound

- Matrix

- MicroPub

- NeoDb

- Outbound

- OStatus

- SMTP

- WebMention

- XMPP

- Zot

We already covered ActivityPub and OStatus; other than those, three others are used by the top five number of nodes:

- Diaspora

- DFRN

- Matrix

Diaspora

Diaspora has its own protocol for decentralized, social networking. It was developed in 2010, based on a federated architecture similar to email (with inbox and outbox, also similar to ActivityPub) allowing users to share data and communicate with each other across a network of multiple independent nodes, called "pods" (no direct relation to Kubernetes pods, although some Diaspora pods may well run in Kubernetes clusters). Besides Diaspora itself, the protocol is also used by Friendica or Hubzilla.

DFRN

DFRN is a distributed communication protocol that provides privacy and secure communications as well as a foundation for distributed profiles and connections like friend requests.

Matrix

Matrix was initially developed as a protocol for secure, decentralized instant messaging at Amdocs, provider of CRM and Telecom solutions like OSS or BSS. Use cases include voice over IP, video chat, or secure IoT.

The features of Matrix include the following:

- Creation and management of fully distributed chat rooms with no single points of control or failure

- Eventually consistent cryptographically secure synchronization of room state across a global open network of federated servers

- Sending and receiving extensible messages in a room with optional end-to-end encryption

- User management

  - Inviting

  - Joining

  - Leaving

  - Kicking out, banning

  - Mediated by a power user

- Room state management

  - Naming

  - Aliasing

  - Topics

  - Bans

- User profile management (avatars, display names, etc.)

- Managing user accounts (registration, login, logout)

- Use of third-party IDs like email address, phone number, Facebook accounts, or other social IDs to authenticate, identify, and discover users on Matrix

- Identity federation

  - Publishing user public keys for PKI

  - Mapping of third-party IDs to Matrix IDs

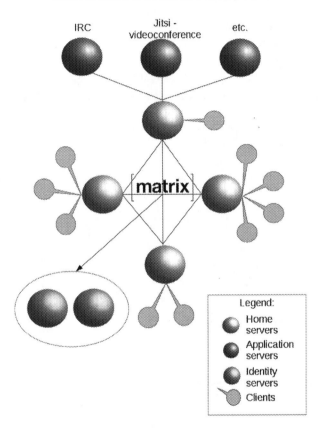

Figure 3-6. *Matrix Network Architecture*

Adoption

Matrix is used widely by government agencies around the world, particularly in Europe, with stricter data security and privacy regulations.

Rocket Chat is based on Matrix since version 4.7.0. In 2021 and 2022, the FOSDEM conference was hosted using Matrix.

There are official Matrix bridges for

- Gitter

- IRC

- Slack/Mattermost

- XMPP

And several other bridges maintained by the community for

- Apple iMessage

- Discord

- Email

- Facebook Messenger

- LinkedIn

- Mastodon

- Signal

- Skype

- SMS

- Telegram

- WeChat

- WhatsApp

Java Frameworks and Libraries

Following Java standards like Portlet API or various parts of Enterprise Java, there have been several Java frameworks and libraries for social media.

Facebook Business SDK for Java

The Facebook (Meta) Business SDK is a one-stop solution to help partners and customers with their enterprise social solutions, allowing partners to use multiple

Facebook APIs like Pages, Business Manager, Instagram, etc., to serve their business needs. Common features include the following:

- Ads buying – Guide for creating ad campaigns for Click-to-Messenger Ads and promoting your Facebook page

- Instagram management – Guide for publishing photos and responding to comments on Instagram

- Onboarding clients at scale – Guide for managing hundreds or thousands of small businesses and offering them ads buying within their website or platform

- Page management – Guide to creating pages, updating pages, and managing their content

Here is a quick start example; see `https://github.com/facebook/facebook-java-business-sdk`.

```java
import com.facebook.ads.sdk.APIContext;
import com.facebook.ads.sdk.AdAccount;
import com.facebook.ads.sdk.AdAccount.EnumCampaignStatus;
import com.facebook.ads.sdk.AdAccount.EnumCampaignObjective;
import com.facebook.ads.sdk.Campaign;
import com.facebook.ads.sdk.APIException;

public class QuickStartExample {

  public static final String ACCESS_TOKEN = "[Your access token]";
  public static final Long ACCOUNT_ID = [Your account ID];
  public static final String APP_SECRET = "[Your app secret]";

  public static final APIContext context = new APIContext(ACCESS_TOKEN,
  APP_SECRET);
  public static void main(String[] args) {
    try {
      AdAccount account = new AdAccount(ACCOUNT_ID, context);
      Campaign campaign = account.createCampaign()
        .setName("Java SDK Test Campaign")
        .setObjective(Campaign.EnumObjective.VALUE_LINK_CLICKS)
```

```
        .setSpendCap(10000L)
        .setStatus(Campaign.EnumStatus.VALUE_PAUSED)
        .execute();
      System.out.println(campaign.fetch());
    } catch (APIException e) {
      e.printStackTrace();
    }
  }
}
```

We will show more examples on using the Facebook/Meta Business SDK for Java in Chapter 6.

After the first pre-release in May 2016, Facebook has constantly maintained its Java SDK besides developer support for JavaScript (Node.js), PHP, Ruby, or Python. The most recent version is v16.0.1, released in March 2023 with a release cycle not so different from Spring, JBoss/Red Hat, or the JDK itself, getting new major versions twice a year.

Twitter4J

Twitter4J is an unofficial Java library for the Twitter API. With Twitter4J, you can easily integrate Twitter calls in your Java application.

Its author, Yusuke Yamamoto, used to work for Twitter in 2012.

While he did, he was briefly meant to represent Twitter in the Social JSR Expert Group, more on that under JSR 357 later in this chapter.

It's lightweight, still backward-compatible with Java 8, making it also easy to integrate into mobile or embedded apps for instance. Not very surprising, more or less official clones and forks or projects inspired by it are available anywhere from J2ME to Android. Twitter4J is an API Binding Library, thus primarily for consuming information. While extensions or your application could analyze or transform it, the framework itself doesn't provide support beyond that of Twitter itself. Based on Hinchcliffe's categorization, Twitter4J could mostly be seen as a Basic API, but with aspects of higher order.

The last version was 4.1.2 in October 2022. After a longer break between 2018 and 2022, it now seems reasonably well maintained again. A risk, however, is that Twitter4J so far only supports Twitter API v1.1, and with the whole Elon Musk situation at Twitter, nobody knows for sure if and how long both will be available. On the other hand, with Twitter's workforce decimated to just a mere shadow of pre-Musk times, it is unlikely all services are going to be migrated to v2 only in just a few weeks. And with a Premium v1.1 API offering some revenue, it isn't likely going away overnight without granting paying users a time to migrate to v2 equivalents. While Gnip has been purchased by Twitter nearly ten years ago, the Enterprise API is only being rebranded from Gnip 2.0 very recently, and that process may also be hampered by all the developers with experience Musk either fired or made leave Twitter on their own.

Here's an example of how to sign in with Twitter4J.

Sign in with Twitter:

```java
import twitter4j.*;
import twitter4j.v1.Status;

class Main {
    public static void main(String[] args) throws Exception {
        long userId = Long.parseLong(args[0]);
        String accessToken = loadAccessToken(userId);
        String accessTokenSecret = loadAccessTokenSecret(userId);
        Twitter twitter = Twitter.newBuilder()
                .oAuthConsumer("[consumer key]", "[consumer secret]")
                .oAuthAccessToken(accessToken, accessTokenSecret).build();
        Status status = twitter.v1().tweets().updateStatus(args[1]);
        System.out.println("Successfully updated the status to
        [%s].".formatted(status.getText()));
        System.exit(0);
    }

    private static String loadAccessToken(long userId) {
        return "[token]"; // load from a persistent store
    }

    private static String loadAccessTokenSecret(long userId) {
        return "[token secret]"; // load from a persistent store
    }
}
```

We will show more examples of how to use Twitter4J in Chapter 6.

Twitter API Client Library for Java

In August 2021, Twitter started its own API client library for Java [35]. Quite late, but supporting the Twitter v2 API only, it was meant to convince developers to migrate to the new API.

Until 2021 Twitter had been a very active and welcoming JCP Executive Committee member, hosting more face-to-face meetings in its HQ than any other JCP member except maybe Sun and later Oracle. Twitter was also an active committer to OpenJDK and maintained its own version of the JDK optimized for performance and scalability. So it wasn't so surprising Twitter also offered a Java client library although it came a bit late and the readme file in the GitHub repo still says "This SDK is in beta and is not ready for production".

While used by over 100 other GitHub projects and likely also some commercial users, there were only three contributors; all must have worked at Twitter, while only one committer in New Zealand still seems affiliated with the Twitter development team, although his contribution stopped in the very early stage of the library. Another one is also based in New Zealand and just left Twitter in February 2023, seemingly a Musk fall-out. He also created a fork of Twitter4J and probably studied it quite a bit, although there seem to be no PRs back to Twitter4J. Time will tell if he may also contribute to it. The last contribution came by the co-founder of a French electromobility startup named Recharger Mon Auto in Summer 2022, around the time of the Twitter takeover by Elon Musk. Although the committer has no direct work relationship with Tesla, the timing indicates he might be from Elon's orbit and was asked to look at the code, or at least his company has such a vital interest in using Twitter APIs that he got involved.

The last contribution was in October 2022 just when the Musk takeover was finalized, and there has not been any code commit since.

Here's a "Hello World" example for the Twitter API client library; see `https://github.com/twitterdev/twitter-api-java-sdk`.

```
package com.twitter.clientlib;

import java.util.HashSet;
import java.util.Set;
import com.twitter.clientlib.TwitterCredentialsBearer;
import com.twitter.clientlib.ApiException;
import com.twitter.clientlib.api.TwitterApi;
import com.twitter.clientlib.model.*;
```

```java
public class HelloWorld {

  public static void main(String[] args) {
    /**
     * Set the credentials for the required APIs.
     * The Java SDK supports TwitterCredentialsOAuth2 & TwitterCredentialsBearer.
     * Check the 'security' tag of the required APIs in https://api.
     twitter.com/2/openapi.json in order
     * to use the right credential object.
     */
    TwitterApi apiInstance = new TwitterApi(new
    TwitterCredentialsBearer(System.getenv("TWITTER_BEARER_TOKEN")));

    Set<String> tweetFields = new HashSet<>();
    tweetFields.add("author_id");
    tweetFields.add("id");
    tweetFields.add("created_at");

    try {
     // findTweetById
     Get2TweetsIdResponse result = apiInstance.tweets().findTweetById("20")
      .tweetFields(tweetFields)
      .execute();
     if(result.getErrors() != null && result.getErrors().size() > 0) {
       System.out.println("Error:");

       result.getErrors().forEach(e -> {
         System.out.println(e.toString());
         if (e instanceof ResourceUnauthorizedProblem) {
           System.out.println(((ResourceUnauthorizedProblem) e).getTitle()
           + " " + ((ResourceUnauthorizedProblem) e).getDetail());
         }
       });
     } else {
       System.out.println("findTweetById - Tweet Text: " + result.
       toString());
     }
```

```
    } catch (ApiException e) {
      System.err.println("Status code: " + e.getCode());
      System.err.println("Reason: " + e.getResponseBody());
      System.err.println("Response headers: " + e.getResponseHeaders());
      e.printStackTrace();
    }
  }
}
```

It remains to be seen if the API ever graduates from Beta, but given the main committer no longer works there and the general cost-saving efforts by Twitter under Musk, that seems unlikely.

We will show more examples of how to use the Twitter API in Chapter 6.

Apache Shindig

Apache Shindig [19] was started relatively soon after the OpenSocial [15] efforts began. Mainly driven by Google and its Orkut at first for obvious reasons, other contributors, especially IBM, joined later. Due to the refocus of OpenSocial toward a "Social Intranet," none of the sites or software claimed to use it are sure to still do so. In fact, Google Partuza points to a nonexisting page; hence, it was shut down like other examples we heard of earlier.

An interesting approach by Google to develop OpenSocial applications inside a WYSIWYG environment of Eclipse IDE was OpenSocial Development Environment (OSDE); see [20]. It is safe to assume some were taken over by IBM and integrated into social editions of Eclipse-based development tools like RAD, etc. while the Google Code project was last updated in June 2010.

OpenSocial API specifications linked to by Apache Shindig are no longer hosted even by OpenSocial supporter Atlassian; it seems the link points to an error page. Whether or not this means Atlassian also doesn't believe in OpenSocial and won't use it in newer versions of its products or it's simply a process of reviving the whole OpenSocial movement on W3C remains to be seen. In the meantime, all versions of OpenSocial, especially 1.0 or 2.0, have been failures, and sites like Orkut at most used the 0.7 or 0.8 version. According to OpenSocial supporting Dachis Group [16], Shindig as manifestation represents a basic standard (2c). It has means of both providing and consuming information.

On September 30, 2014, Google shut down Orkut, making Google+, which it also discontinued in 2019, the only remaining Google reference at the time. By 2015, still over 20 social networks integrated OpenSocial, among them StudiVZ, MySpace, LinkedIn, or XING, but soon after, most social media providers have gradually abandoned it.

Google had already stopped using Shindig in favor of its own Google Code projects. Most of them were also closed down and either point to the OpenSocial page now, or no longer exist. So on October 23, 2015, Apache Foundation retired the Shindig project. After that with the de facto Reference Implementation of OpenSocial discontinued, it also followed its fate.

Efforts by Sun/Oracle

Around 2008, Enterprise Social Mashup driver BEA Systems [13] had just been acquired by Oracle; Java creator Sun Microsystems did not quite guess a similar fate was also around the corner for it. Based on OpenSocial, Sun created a fork or derived project from Apache Shindig named SocialSite [21].

SocialSite still counts 231 members on java.net, but the project is inactive. One of the last commits was by Kohsuke Kawaguchi, Sun's creator of Hudson CI server and later Jenkins after he was hired by CloudBees.

Following the acquisition of RightNow Technologies (see [23] end of 2011), maker of SaaS CRM software with social aspects – a move clearly targeting the likes of Salesforce.com or SAP – some of the former RightNow teams and products were incorporated into Oracle's social enabled enterprise department.

JavaOne 2012 featured a Social Day I also attended with speakers like Facebook's Developer Relations Manager James Pearce. Oracle itself presented a "one man" project written by a freelance contractor still for RightNow under the code name "Project Sneaker," which just after JavaOne 2012 was published as Oracle SocialLink [24].

It never attracted followers outside Oracle and had to be considered deader than even SocialSite.

DaliCore

After Oracle took over Sun, the abandoned SocialSite found its best equivalent and successor in DaliCore [22].

It was originally based on a CMS made by a Belgian start-up, mainly around BeJUG (Devoxx conferences) members like Johan Vos. DaliCMS (2006) was called a "Web 2.0 ready CMS"

It was mostly an open source project with community features. In 2008, around the same time Sun did with SocialSite, support for Shindig was added to DaliCMS, mostly JavaScript code from Shindig and some Java code provided by DaliCMS.

Eventually it became more than a CMS, and the underlying modules turned into DaliCore. During his talk at JavaOne 2013, Johan unveiled the origin of the "Dali" part, which stood for "Dutch Amazon Lovers Initiative" – a tribute to Internet and Cloud pioneer Amazon.

DaliCore added functionality common to user management, content, or permissions on top of Java EE 6, with a strong focus on users and permissions. In about every project that uses DaliCore, users should be able to log in with existing credentials (Facebook, Twitter, Google+, LinkedIn, etc.). So-called Dali modules extended DaliCore. While certain connectivity exists to social providers like Facebook, these mainly serve as authentication providers to DaliCore SSO (Single Sign-On) functionality. Aside from that, DaliCore aims at providing information.

Important aspects of DaliCore were as follows:

- Mostly social container and CMS with partial open social features.

- Java Persistence support via EJB, JPA, or similar standards.

- No clear separation of modules, especially API/Spec and Implementation, in most cases shares the same module and even package space, making reuse and extension harder despite the attempt for that via Dali Module.

- Seemed a bit heavy, strong dependency on the Full Java EE profile, that is, using only its Web Profile looked harder.

- GlassFish support and integration are positive where it is the preferred application server. Thanks to the Java EE standard, it is not impossible but seems harder to use with other containers.

- It demonstrated scalability also under heavy usage with some customers, for example, an e-voting site in Belgium. Unlike Apache Shindig or Sun SocialSite (which DaliCore seems like a natural successor in most cases), it is used by actual customers at least in Benelux countries.

After Oracle announced it will no longer provide commercial support for GlassFish or enhanced features like clustering (beyond PoC quality provided by a Java EE Reference Implementation, it'll remain), performance tuning, etc., a major argument for DaliCore vanished. Oracle recommends its WebLogic/Fusion Middleware products, or current GlassFish users will be forced to migrate to other servers if they need commercial support.

DaliCore author Johan Vos and his Belgian start-up then claim they'd offer commercial support for their customers and maybe even try to extend that, but DaliCore has become a clear victim of this. Since early 2013, there has been no activity in the java.net repository, and after Oracle closed java.net in 2017, none of it was migrated elsewhere, at least not to a publicly available site. While Johan Vos told us back then he was still working on it, he also confirmed this was done in a private repository at Bitbucket. Thus, DaliCore never became open source again and must now be considered dead.

Spring Social

SpringSource, which had been rebranded by its parent companies as Pivotal before ultimately becoming part of VMware again, has a long history of jumping on trends and providing libraries or extensions to its Spring Framework for just about everything.

Spring Social [25] is a binding library for consuming information. Although integrating OAuth with Spring Security and other parts is symptomatic of a Basic API, it shows more aspects of a Higher-Order API than most other solutions mentioned here.

Important aspects of Spring Social are as follows:

- It works primarily with Spring Framework or other parts of the Spring landscape for obvious reasons.

- UI frameworks other than Spring MVC are relatively harder to integrate.

- Official Spring Social connectors focused mostly on Facebook; examples only showed Single Service approach.

- Despite an otherwise lively Spring community, it's no longer actively supported.

- There were just one, two at most active committers and drivers behind Spring Social, employed by a single company.

We will show more about Spring Social in Chapter 6.

Microsoft Embedded Social

Microsoft Embedded Social [34], established on May 15, 2012, was a multi-tenant cloud service for social user engagement inside applications. While mostly a research project, its project page claims it was used at times by over 20 million users.

It aimed at an abstraction across multiple social networks, a bit like other similar efforts like OpenSocial, Seam Social, Spring Social, or Agorava.

server architecture

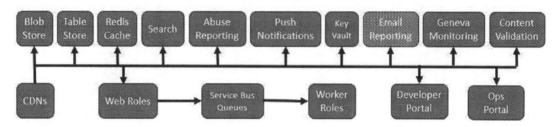

Figure 3-7. *Embedded Social Server Architecture*

Its features include

- User authentication
- User profiles
- Topics
- Expressions
- Social graph
- Dynamic feeds
- Content moderation
- Search
- Popular and recent

Other than usage for LinkedIn, which Microsoft had purchased in 2016, Embedded Social seemed mostly academic, similar to Google's 20% projects, and although there were still publications until around 2020, the project seems more or less inactive and abandoned now.

Seam Social

Seam Social was part of the JBoss Seam 3 project offering social connectivity on top of Java EE standards like CDI [28]. Seam Social is a binding library for consuming information. While OAuth on top of CDI and Java EE can be considered a Basic API, Seam Social was the richest Higher-Order API before Agorava, especially by providing CDI events for social behavior such as likes, check-ins, or updates to a user's Timeline. Common API bindings in most cases dictated by a provider's API definition or sometimes directly generated from it were inspired by Spring Social, but Seam Social was never a clone or fork, as it stands to Spring Social like underlying CDI and extensions do to Spring Framework.

In early 2012, Seam was stopped to be merged with Apache DeltaSpike, which was a reason for Seam Social to move on as well ... becoming Agorava [33].

JSR 357

Between JavaOne 2011 and further conferences like Devoxx in Antwerp, I initiated a series of discussions with CDI Spec Lead Pete Muir, Twitter4J author Yusuke Yamamoto, or Seam Social creator Antoine Sabot-Durand to explore a possible standardization of social media APIs for the Java platform in the Java Community Process.

They thought it was an idea worth pursuing. Other APIs and projects like DaliCore were considered possibly relevant (especially providing information under Java EE) due to the strong use of CDI and rather well-structured separation of API and implementation made Seam Social the best candidate for initial code base.

The JSR was proposed by me and Antoine as co-Spec Leads, joined by companies like Red Hat/JBoss, eXo Platform, or Twitter (represented by Twitter4J creator Yusuke Yamamoto) as well as JUG Chennai, DaliCore authors from BeJUG or Java EE 7 EG Member, and Oracle ACE director Markus Eisele (now again working at Red Hat, like Antoine did till 2021), a healthy mix of corporate individuals and JUGs one might say.

However, after IBM first voted against the JSR, other EC members like SAP followed, one JUG (SouJava) voted in favor, the other (LJC) voted against it, and the creation ballot ended 8 against 5, stopping the creation of JSR 357. Sadly, although with big vendors preferring "walled gardens" [14] over open standards, not entirely surprising, even interested party and EG member candidate Twitter abstained. See [26] for an article about the ballot.

IBM felt strong about OpenSocial, but as even some of its other supporters like Adjuvi's Dion Hinchcliffe [16] explained (a bit later though), OpenSocial is a Basic Standard while the main goal of JSR 357 following Seam Social was to offer a Higher-Order API and binding to the Java platform. Take WebSockets, among the JSRs 357 mentioned having potential for synergies. The W3C standard just along the lines of OpenSocial successors was defined under the HTML5 umbrella, while the Oracle JSR creates a Java implementation. Even on the Java platform, there have been several existing, well-adopted open source projects for WebSockets; nevertheless, it was found worth creating a JSR, too. Similar for JSON and maybe even more striking as the de facto Reference Implementation by JSON "father" Douglas Crockford inspired the JSON JSR, but Crockford while initially "supporting this JSR" told me personally at Dutch Mobile Conference last year he no longer intended to be involved and has never stopped supporting and promoting his own libraries around it.

The fact that first opposing IBM sold hundreds, maybe thousands of Social Media Software Patents to Facebook the week JSR 357 was voted down doesn't just present a bad optic. It also makes IBM's own support of OpenSocial a bit questionable if social media patents and proprietary technologies are sold to Facebook, bolstering its arsenal against competitors like Twitter and others. It could be a reason behind Twitter's "mood swing" at the last moment of the ballot. Maybe a coincidence, but Twitter4J author Yusuke Yamamoto left Twitter soon after that. Whether or not EC members like IBM or SAP didn't want Red Hat in an influential role in more key open source projects after Hibernate, CDI/Seam, or Arquillian, just to name a few, it could have been another reason, too. Especially on that one I'd say if it was among intentions, it backfired with the creation and active development of Agorava, not just by one company (like DaliCore or Social Link) but a variety of contributors around the world, most of them proposed EG members.

Killing a likely heir to the Java Social "throne," especially with a significant French participation one may say, created a "French Revolution" of Java Social Frameworks named Agorava.

You'll hear more about Agorava in Chapter 6.

Summary

In this chapter, we learned about different kinds of social standards and the efforts to standardize interaction with social networks, allowing some level of provider neutrality as well as cross-platform publication.

CHAPTER 4

Social Security

The surge of cybersecurity attacks has nowadays created the need for defending our organization on multiple security fronts, be it physical, technological, or policies and procedures. Each one of the aforementioned fronts is equally important to your organization's security. None of them should be undermined toward creating a future-proof and secure organization. That is, having only physical security is not enough. Having only physical and technical security could indeed be somewhat more challenging to hackers, yet if your employees are not well educated to protect their passwords, your organization isn't very secure overall.

Information security is based on

- Confidentiality

- Integrity

- Availability

These three concepts are often referred to as the CIA Triad. It formed over time and does not have a single creator. Confidentiality was first proposed as early as 1976 in a study by the US Air Force; the concept of integrity was explored in a 1987 paper titled "A Comparison of Commercial and Military Computer Security Policies" written by David Clark and David Wilson [55].

The paper recognized that commercial computing had a need for accounting records and data correctness. Even though it is not as easy to find an initial source, the concept of availability became more widespread a year later, in 1988. Another ten years later, by 1998, people saw the three concepts together as the CIA Triad.

> Confidentiality – Information should not be read by unauthorized users.

> Integrity – Information should not be able to be falsified unnoticed.

© Werner Keil 2024
W. Keil, *Enterprise Social for the Java Platform*, https://doi.org/10.1007/978-1-4842-9571-7_4

For example, a hacker should not be able to seize and modify any data before it's sent to the intended recipient.

> Availability – Requires that information is accessible whenever authorized users need it.

In addition to the CIA Triad, there are some more key concepts of social media security:

- Confidentiality

- Integrity

- Availability

- Privacy

- Authentication

- Authorization

Privacy – Users can control the access, use, and disclosure of their personal information. Privacy is the concept of maintaining secrecy, anonymity, and freedom from surveillance or intrusion into one's private matters. Privacy can be understood as the power to control when, how, and to what extent personal information is shared with others.

Under the CCPA, personal information is "information that identifies, relates to, describes, is reasonably capable of being associated with, or could reasonably be linked, directly or indirectly, with a particular consumer or household."

Under the GDPR, personal information is termed as "personal data," which is considered "any information related to an identified or identifiable natural person."

Authentication – Users can prove they are who they say they are, their **identity**; for example, a client can prove to a server that they are acting on behalf of an authorized identity and vice versa. Or the caller ID of an incoming call.

Authorization – Users have enough permissions to access restricted resources or perform specific operations.

Authentication and authorization are sometimes confused nowadays, so here's a good way to remember how these two terms are different in the world of identity and access management (IAM). Authentication confirms that users are who they say they are, whereas authorization permits those users to access a resource.

Privacy

The term privacy comes from "private" and has Latin origin: "prīvātus," which literally means taken away from public affairs.

While ancient Romans may have been able to hide some of their affairs from public audience and famous writers of their time, and the time from something actually happening to being written down and consumed by readers was at least days, more often months or even years, it can sometimes be just the blink of an eye or click of a mouse button today.

The revelations by whistleblower Edward Snowden were the most extensive but certainly not the first case of privacy concerns brought into public light especially with regard to social networks or similar online services [37]. The ability to combine data from various sources and everyday life aspects into a digital picture and footprint of users was in prior decades mostly the domain of police and secret service tools like "Dragnet" (not so much the movie, though it referred to the system in a humorous way).

Not just Snowden and his skills now available to his hosts in Russia is a clear indicator Western countries and agencies aren't the only ones interested in such information. Many try to control; some simply block or restrict entire services, if they are not provided the same access to vital information by the social networks as intelligence agencies in their home country, usually the United States, China, Russia, or Turkey, the list keeps growing of countries temporarily or permanently blocking some providers. If ownership or hosting is outsourced, not for tax but cheap workforce reasons, then some services can be affected by practices in these countries, too. One of the most popular examples we heard about earlier, because OpenID 1.0 was once created there, is LiveJournal. In 2007, it was sold by Six Apart to the Russian Media group SUP Media in December 2007.

After 2009, most of its production was also moved to Russia, and employees were fired in Silicon Valley. Although privately owned, SUP Media is clearly controlled and also censored by Russian secret services. For example, in 2007, Russian blogger Savva Terentyev was accused of fomenting social hatred to the staff of the Ministry of Internal Affairs and sentenced to one year probation due to his comment in the blog of a local journalist. Not to mention recent murders like that of regime-critical Boris Nemtsov in Moscow only hours after he had announced to disclose information on Russia's involvement in Ukraine and the 2014 occupation of Crimea. Ironically Even in one of the most tightly censored countries like Russia, there was a tiny glimpse of hope, that Social media if not bring real reforms may at least help finding clues to his murder [38].

Furthermore, since Russia started a full-blown war against Ukraine in early 2022, many Russian soldiers could be attacked by Ukrainian forces, because they disclosed their whereabouts on social media or dating sites.

While the argument of "National Security" and trying to catch terrorists or severe criminals online was used to justify mass surveillance on a global scale, critical bloggers or journalists often risk not just their privacy but lives if their identity is unveiled to people and agencies they criticize.

Although efforts like the "Vorratsdatenspeicherung" by European hosting providers and other Internet or mobile companies mean there isn't total privacy in Europe either, most EU countries, especially Germany, have rather strong privacy and data protection laws compared to the United States and many other parts of the world. A few countries like Iceland (not currently in the EU, but EFTA) have even stronger data protection laws, as well as many Scandinavian countries.

Social networks based in these countries, for example, German XING but also Deutsche Telekom and other Internet companies from Germany like GMX/1&1, claim their data is safe from direct access by NSA or other spies. Although local and international inquiries will be executed by these if probable cause exists against a user of serious offenses like murder, terror, organized crime, or child pornography, neither of these services are likely to conduct mass screenings of every single user on a daily basis like NSA and other agencies do in the United States and other countries. Without a warrant to access records or pre-emptively snoop into communication, most European users should feel safe if the provider and its servers are all genuinely based in Europe and data isn't sent via connections abroad.

Privacy Breaches

These are the top ten social media sites losing most user data in privacy breaches:

1. Yahoo! – Over 3.5bn users were affected by data and privacy breaches at Yahoo, including the biggest single breach involving 3bn users in 2013.

2. Facebook – Over 2.1bn users were affected by more than eight data breaches since Facebook was founded in 2004, including the Cambridge Analytica scandal that was not exactly losing data but selling information about at least 87m users. Four breaches in 2019 alone pushed the number of users Facebook had data stolen or mishandled past 2bn.

3. LinkedIn – Most of the 1.1bn LinkedIn accounts affected by data breaches occurred in 2021 when details about 700m were sold on the dark web.

4. MySpace – Three breaches exposed the data of 719m MySpace users.

5. Sina Weibo – Data about 539m users of the Chinese social network, including 172m phone numbers, were offered on the dark web in 2020.

6. Twitter – Twitter confirmed in June 2023 that a hacker had gained access to user details of 5.4m accounts. Bringing the total number of affected accounts to 370m, more than the active users of "X" nowadays.

7. Quora – 100m passwords and security questions were exposed by a 2018 hack.

8. Dailymotion – In 2016, a hacker stole over 85m email addresses, usernames, and passwords from the video sharing platform Dailymotion.

9. Tumblr – Also in 2016, Tumblr announced its security and user privacy were compromised three years earlier, in 2013, and account details of 65m users had been stolen.

10. Instagram – At least 49m users of Meta-owned Instagram were exposed to a privacy breach in 2019, when an unprotected server was hacked.

Little surprising, except Dailymotion, based in France, and Sina Weibo from China, all others are from the United States, where surveillance is omnipresent and privacy is often handled laxly. The fact that Twitter/X rival Threads by Meta had no full rollout to the EU yet is also related to data protection and privacy laws over here in Europe and likely past large-scale data breaches there as well.

In addition to originating in the EU, services like XING also offer much finer-grained levels of access permissions and control by its users, where it is possible to sometimes restrict, for example, who can see each individual data item. Let's say you want to show your name and day of birth, but not the year or your age to everyone visiting your profile, or allow only your friends to see your phone number; this and more can be controlled by systems like XING.

This was also among the reasons why XING abandoned OpenSocial, because it cannot offer such fine-grained access control or in some cases won't even provide any but instead show everything to everyone or at least all data to all of your friends.

Most standards and protocols that succeeded OpenSocial via W3C or others used on the Fediverse are also not always a good fit for privacy, but there are a few, especially Matrix which put a great focus on security and privacy (remember from the previous chapter, Matrix was originally created at Amdocs in Israel) and is therefore trusted by NGOs as well as government agencies around the world.

Diaspora is also strong about privacy, which is why some extremists like the Islamist group ISIS flocked there in 2014, after other larger social networks like Twitter had censored or suspended their accounts. Being a distributed service with high privacy standards, it was not trivial in the absence of a central point of control, monitoring or blocking content, but by August 2014, the Diaspora Foundation stated that via community moderation and word of mouth by the community, all of its larger pods had removed ISIS content and accounts.

Elon Musk got a young man, Jack Sweeney, who (based on fandom or curiosity) tracked his flights on Twitter kicked off the network, just a few days after his Twitter takeover, claiming it would "dox" him (share information about someone, often the location). The young man moved to Mastodon among other social networks like Instagram. Of course the same Elon Musk regularly tweets from public appearances like the Qatar 2022 World Cup Final and similar occasions.

Now X, formerly Twitter led by Elon Musk, plans to start storing users' biometric data, as well as their employment and education history. There is no explanation why they want to store biometrics. Passkey Authentication (we'll hear more about that later in this chapter, but PayPal, the company Elon Musk started his fortune with, as an early adopter) done properly won't exchange biometric information. It only remains in the device. So a more likely reason could be that Musk plans something similar to Worldcoin by OpenAI's co-founder Sam Altman, which involves biometric verification. The planned collection of employment and education history is said to be related to plans for "X Hire," a sort of competitor to LinkedIn or XING under the "X" umbrella, but Musk being a close ally of Ron DeSantis and his "anti-woke" crusade, where teachers who teach "something wrong" are often discriminated or fired in Florida and elsewhere, puts a rather scary note behind this intention. So does Musk's old PayPal buddy and co-founder Peter Thiel, who further grew his fortune at Facebook and played a dubious role in its Cambridge Analytica data breach scandal with his "data octopus" Palantir.

The reported plans to remove the blocking feature from X also do not make many users comfortable, and it certainly would be a blow to privacy and safety in the network. While blocking an unwanted account hides everything you say and do from them, the mute feature just hides their posts from you, but they or the hackers and troll farms behind them can still see anything about your profile. From cyber-stalking to political and racial harassment, this would further open a door for bad actors on the network formerly known as Twitter.

Authentication

Like the word "Agora," authentication is also derived from Greek terms. Originally from Greek "afthentikós," it was a derivative of the noun "authentes," "doer, master," which was formed from "autos," "self," and the base -hentes, "worker, doer, being."

As *authentication*, we define the process of verifying someone's identity. In other words, authentication is all about proving that you're indeed the person or the system you claim to be. Ok, let's make this rather professional definition a bit easier to understand by pulling our beloved fictitious characters: Alice and Bob. Suppose Alice wants to send a message to Bob. How could Bob be sure that he is indeed texting with Alice and not with someone who claims to be Alice? There are basically three different ways Bob could use to verify Alice's identity: by something she knows, something she has, or something she is.

Authenticating someone's identity may be a result of one or more of three types of methods:

1. Something you know

2. Something you have

3. Something you are

Something You Know

We classify information as *something you know* if we store it in our memory and retrieve it when needed. We can identify *something you know* authentication methods in our daily interaction by taking a look at almost any system where we have to authenticate ourselves to interact with: our bank account, our email address, our social media accounts, etc. Yes, you got it right, the most common *something you know* authentication methods are passwords, secret codes, passphrases, and personal identification numbers (PINs).

The *something you know* authentication is the most commonly used authentication method due to its low cost and easy implementation. However, its easy implementation has some side effects, one of which is that it may not be considered strong authentication. Moreover, the *something you know* authentication alone is not enough for applications or systems that require high security.

Something You Have

The *something you have* authentication method refers to something that the user has. Did you notice one major drawback the *something you know* method has? It's all about our memory and its (limited) capacity; that is, passwords can easily be forgotten. The *something you have* method removes that problem, as it's all about some object that must be with you whenever you want to authenticate yourself. Again, here it's all about possessing some kind of token.

Examples of *something you have* authentication could be a credit card, a USB stick, or an OTP card. Of course, carrying an authentication object with you entails its risks – they may be stolen, damaged, or lost.

Something You Are

The *something you are* authentication method addresses what the user *is* and mainly refers to biometric authentication methods. Simply put, biometrics are any metrics related to human features that theoretically can be used for identification or verification of identity. There are various biometric data types such as facial recognition, fingerprints, iris and retina recognition, voice recognition, vein recognition, DNA, and digital signatures.

Biometrics can distinguish one person from another.

How does biometrics compare to the other two authentication methods? It's less well understood than the *something you know* and *something you have* methods, yet it can significantly contribute to the strength of authentication when used correctly in addition to the other two methods.

We consider strong authentication the use of two or more different authentication methods, such as a smart card and a PIN, or a password and a form of biometrics such as a fingerprint, voice, or iris recognition.

Latest Trends in Authentication

Is that all? We can only use three authentication methods to secure our systems?

Of course not. As hackers are becoming smarter, there is a need for additional (and more sophisticated) authentication methods, including *somewhere you are* and *something you do.*

Somewhere you are is related to your location and supports two different flavors: *geolocation security checks* where the location of the user is checked against the configured location of their account and *MAC address checks* where, for example, an employee who is trying to access the company network from a different machine will not be granted any access due to a different MAC address.

Something you do is the least popular authentication method. This kind of authentication is all about verifying a user by observing their actions (touches or gestures). An example here could be the *picture password* feature Windows 8 comes with, which allows you to configure touches and gestures on a picture as a way to authenticate yourself. A more common tech-savvy example of *something you do* to authenticate yourself is your smartphone's gesture authentication, where you use your thumb to swipe a gesture pattern on your smartphone's screen so you can unlock it.

Passkey Authentication

Passkeys allow you to sign in securely to services like social networks, without having to enter a password.

Unlike security keys, passkeys have the benefit of being user-verifying. This means passkeys verify your identity using "something you know" or "something you are," like a PIN or biometric check (such as a fingerprint, iris, or facial recognition), or a pattern, for example, a QR code.

History

The idea of passkeys first came up in 2009, when Validity Sensors, later acquired by Synaptics, and PayPal joined forces on the concept of using biometrics instead of passwords for online identification. Together with several other IT leaders, they founded the FIDO Alliance, a web security organization, in July 2012. FIDO stands for Fast IDentity Online.

Google joined in 2013. A year later in 2014, PayPal and Samsung started FIDO authentication with the Samsung Galaxy S5 smartphone. Users of the device could authenticate PayPal with the touch of a finger and shop online without having to enter passwords when completing the transaction. The term "passkeys" was popularized just recently, when Apple pushed it at its Worldwide Developers Conference in June 2022, where Apple publicly announced its passkey features in iOS 16 and macOS Ventura.

How Does It Work?

Passkeys are based on the WebAuthn cryptographic protocols developed by the FIDO Alliance. Each passkey is a pair of two related asymmetric cryptographic keys and only works for the website it was created by. The key pair is made up of a private key that's kept on your device, inside a password manager supporting passkeys (the passkey provider), and a public key, stored on the website you want to log into.

You can think of a public key certificate as the digital equivalent of a passport.

Authentication Examples

In this section, we covered some theoretical ground on the basics of authentication. Aren't you yet as excited as we are to see how that plays out in code? Let's look through the Jakarta EE door by examining some basic code snippets for authentication.

In Jakarta EE, the component containers are responsible for providing application security. A container provides two types of security: *declarative* and *programmatic*. Declarative security addresses the use of deployment descriptors or annotations to configure a component's security mechanisms, whereas programmatic security is used by security-aware applications to complement their security model.

Programmatic Authentication

Authenticating users programmatically can be done using the *SecurityContext* and *HttpServletRequest* interfaces.

`SecurityContext`

The Jakarta EE Security API Specification, which you will have the chance to evaluate in the next few chapters, specifies one method to help you trigger an authentication process programmatically:

- authenticate() enables an application to notify the container that it should start the authentication process with the caller.

The HttpServletRequest interface enables you to authenticate web application users programmatically by specifying three simple methods:

- *authenticate* triggers the specific authentication mechanism that has been configured; for example, if that's a form, a login form will be displayed to the user to collect their username and password, whereas if that's simply a social login like "Login with Google," it will redirect the user to Google.

- *login* validates the provided username and password.

- *logout* resets a request's caller identity.

The following code example shows how to use the authenticate method:

```
public class EnterpriseSocialServlet extends HttpServlet {

    protected void processRequest(HttpServletRequest request,
    HttpServletResponse response) throws ServletException, IOException {
        response.setContentType("text/html;charset=UTF-8");
        try (PrintWriter writer = response.getWriter()) {
request.authenticate(response);
            writer.println("Successful authentication!");
        }
    }
}
```

This example shows how to use the *login* and *logout* methods:

```
public class SampleLoginLogoutServlet extends HttpServlet {

protected void processRequest(HttpServletRequest request,
HttpServletResponse response) throws ServletException, IOException {
        response.setContentType("text/html;charset=UTF-8");
        try (PrintWriter out = response.getWriter()) {
```

```
            out.println("<html>");
            out.println("<body>");
            request.login("Chapter4User", "Chapter4User");

            BigDecimal result =
                converterBean.libresToKilos(new BigDecimal("55.0"));

            out.println("<h1>Servlet SampleLoginLogoutServlet result of
            libresToKilos= " + result + "</h1>");
            out.println("</body>");
            out.println("</html>");
        } catch (Exception e) {
            throw new ServletException(e);
        } finally {
            request.logout();
        }
    }
}
```

Authorization

Authorization, also known as access control, is the process of managing access to
resources – in other words, controlling who has access to what in an application.

More formally, to authorize is to define an access policy. Examples of authorization
are: Is a user allowed to look at this web page, read or edit this information, view this
form, or use this printer? Those are all decisions determining what a user may access.

Jakarta Authorization

Java has a security architecture that protects systems from unauthorized access by
mobile/dynamic or static code. The problem is in manually determining the set of
security access rights required to execute a library or application. The commonly used
strategy is to execute the code, note authorization failures, allocate additional access
rights, and test again. This process iterates until the code successfully runs for the
required use cases. Those cases may not always cover all paths through the code, so
failures can occur in deployed systems. On the other hand, a broad set of access rights

may be allocated to the code to prevent authorization failures from occurring. However, this often leads to a violation of the Least Privilege design principle [27].

The Least Privilege design principle requires a minimalistic approach to granting user access rights to specific information and tools. Additionally, access rights should be time based as to limit resources access bound to the time needed to complete necessary tasks. The implications of granting access beyond this scope will allow for unnecessary access and the potential for data to be updated out of the approved context. The assigning of access rights will limit system damaging attacks from users whether they are intentional or not.

Basic Java SE Security relies on **permissions**, for example, `FilePermission` to access the file system or `AWTPermission` to use resources like the clipboard in AWT/Swing applications.

If someone wants to allow a new type of permission for specific applications, this can be done by adding an entry in a policy file.

An example of a policy file entry granting code from the "`http://mysocial.tv/`" permission to watch ARTE would be

```
grant codeBase  "http://mysocial.tv /" {
    permission fr.arte.TVPermission "arte-tv", "watch";
}
```

Security Standards

After we looked at standardized ways to interact with social media in Chapter 3, here are some common standards related to security.

Jakarta Security

Security in Jakarta EE is based on some essential terms:

- User is an individual identity defined in the identity storage. The storage can be a database, flat file, or LDAP server.

- Group is a set of users with the same needs or access levels.

- Security Realm is the access channel for the application server to user and group information.

- Role is a Jakarta EE concept of access levels. A Jakarta EE developer specifies which roles can access which set of application functionalities. These roles are then mapped to users and groups via vendor-specific configuration data.

- Principal is an identity with known credentials that can be authenticated using an authentication protocol.

- Credential contains or references information used to authenticate a principal for Jakarta EE applications, for example, by entering a password, or calling external services. More in "Authentication."

The official scope of Jakarta Security is

Jakarta Security provides a set of required security functionalities including authentication, authorization, data integrity, and transport security.

You'll remember from Chapter 3 that almost every social service or similar API uses RESTful Web Services. REST stands for "Representational State Transfer." Jakarta REST (formerly JAX-RS) is the Jakarta EE API for RESTful Web Services.

Here are some brief examples how authorization can be done by injecting a Jakarta EE SecurityContext instance. The injected security context works on top of lower-level HttpServletRequest API. The injected security context depends on the actual RESTful web application deployment.

SecurityContext can be used in conjunction with subresource locators to return different resources based on the specific roles a user principal is included in, using a CDI @Context annotation [28]. For example, a subresource locator could return a different resource if a user is a "preferred customer."

```
@Path("basket")
public ShoppingBasketResource get(@Context SecurityContext sc) {
    if (sc.isUserInRole("PreferredCustomer") {
        return new PreferredCustomerShoppingBasketResource();
    } else {
        return new ShoppingBasketResource();
    }
}
```

Using SecurityContext for a "resource" endpoint:

```
@Path("resource")
@Singleton
public static class MyResource {
    @Inject
    SecurityContext securityContext;

    @GET
    public String getUserPrincipal() {
        return securityContext.getUserPrincipal().getName();
    }
}
```

by injecting SecurityContext into a singleton resource.

Where a Jakarta REST application is deployed in a Servlet container, you can rely only on the standard Jakarta EE Web application security offered by the Servlet container and configurable via the web.xml descriptor by defining `<security-constraint>` elements in web.xml and assigning roles that are able to access these resources. You can also define HTTP methods allowed to be executed. See the following example:

```
<security-constraint>
    <web-resource-collection>
        <url-pattern>/rest/admin/*</url-pattern>
    </web-resource-collection>
    <auth-constraint>
        <role-name>admin</role-name>
    </auth-constraint>
</security-constraint>
<security-constraint>
    <web-resource-collection>
        <url-pattern>/rest/orders/*</url-pattern>
    </web-resource-collection>
    <auth-constraint>
        <role-name>customer</role-name>
    </auth-constraint>
```

```
</security-constraint>
<login-config>
    <auth-method>BASIC</auth-method>
    <realm-name>my-default-realm</realm-name>
</login-config>
```

Authentication Mechanisms

The Jakarta EE platform supports the following authentication mechanisms:

- Basic authentication

- Form-based authentication

- Custom Form authentication

- Digest authentication

- Client authentication

- OpenID Connect authentication

Everything started with the Servlet specification, which specifies four authentication mechanisms: BASIC, FORM, DIGEST, and CLIENT-CERT. Later, when Jakarta Security API was developed, there was a clear need for BASIC and FORM authentication mechanisms to work the same as their BASIC and FORM counterparts in Servlet specification. That said, we can distinguish five authentication mechanisms overall, of which three come from the Jakarta Security API (BASIC, FORM, CUSTOM-FORM) and two from the Servlet specification (DIGEST, CLIENT).

Now let's have a closer look at each of these.

Basic Authentication

What It Is

Basic authentication is the default authentication when you don't specify any authentication mechanism.

How It Works

The web server requests a username and a password from the web client and verifies that both the username and the password are valid by comparing them against a database of authorized users in the specified or default realm.

In the following, you can see the sequence of actions that occur when basic authentication is used:

1. A web client requests access to a protected recourse.

2. The web server returns a dialog box that requests the username and password.

3. The web client submits the username and password to the server.

4. The server authenticates the user in the specified realm and returns the requested resource upon successful authentication.

Figure 4-1. *Basic Authentication*

How to Configure It

Annotation:

```
package enterprise.social.authentication.mechanism.http;

@Retention(RUNTIME)
@Target(TYPE)
public @interface BasicAuthenticationMechanismDefinition {

    /**
     * Name of realm that will be sent via the <code>WWW-Authenticate</
     code> header.
     * <p>
     * Note that this realm name <b>does not</b> couple a named
     identity store
     * configuration to the authentication mechanism.
     *
```

```
    * @return Name of realm
    */
   String realmName() default "";
}
```

Web.xml:

```
<login-config>
    <auth-method>BASIC</auth-method>
    <realm-name>enterprisesocialbasicrealm</realm-name>
</login-config>
```

Form-Based Authentication

What It Is
An authentication mechanism where the user is presented with an editable form to fill in her login credentials to log into some service or system.

How It Works
The developer controls the *look and feel* of the login screens by customizing the login screen and error pages that an HTTP browser presents to the user.

Let's go through the sequence of actions that occur when form-based authentication is used:

1. A web client requests access to a protected resource.

2. If the client is not authenticated yet, the server redirects them to a login page.

3. The client fills in their username and password and submits the login form to the server.

4. The server attempts to authenticate the user.

5. Authentication

    a. Upon successful authentication, the authenticated user's principal is checked to ensure it belongs to a role being authorized to access the resource. If the user is authorized, the server redirects the client to the resource, using the stored URL.

    b. Upon failed authentication, the client is redirected to an error page.

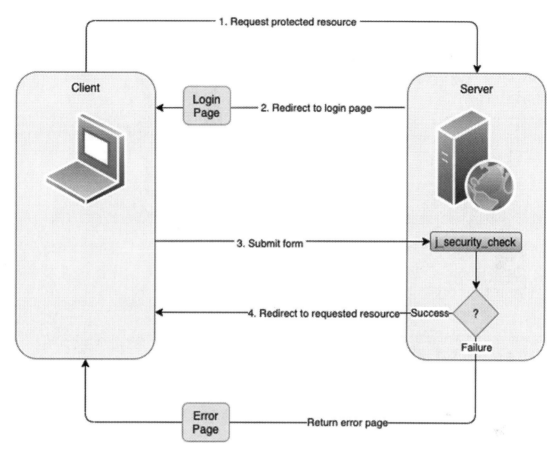

Figure 4-2. *Form-Based Authentication*

For form-based login, make sure to maintain sessions using cookies or TLS session information.

How to Configure It

HTML Form

When working with form-based authentication, be sure to mark your form's action as j_security_check. Thus, the login form will work regardless of which resource it is intended for. Moreover, explicitly declaring this action means for the server that it will not have to specify the action field of the outbound form himself. Here's a code snippet that shows how the HTML form should look like:

```
<form method="POST" action="j_security_check">
<input type="text" name="j_username">
<input type="password" name="j_password">
</form>
```

Annotation:

```
package jakarta.enterprise.social.authentication.mechanism.http;
@Retention(RUNTIME)
@Target(TYPE)
public @interface FormAuthenticationMechanismDefinition {
    @Nonbinding
    LoginToContinue loginToContinue();
}
```

Web.xml:

```
<login-config>
<auth-method>FORM</auth-method>
<form-login-config>
        <form-login-page>/login.xhtml</form-login-page>
        <form-error-page>/error.xhtml</form-error-page>
</form-login-config>
</login-config>
```

Digest Authentication

What It Is

An authentication mechanism similar to the basic authentication, which, however, does not send the password in cleartext. This authentication mechanism intends to avoid the most critical flaws of basic authentication.

How It Works

Just like basic authentication, digest authentication authenticates a user based on a username and a password without providing any encryption of the message. It applies a hash function to the username and password before sending them over the network. That is, passwords are not sent over the wire here, yet it requires cleartext password equivalents to be available to the authenticating container so that it can validate received authenticators by calculating the expected digest.

Application Walkthrough:

1. A client requests access to a protected resource.

2. The server replies with a nonce and a 401 error code.

3. The client sends back a response that contains a checksum (by default, the MD5 checksum) of the username, the password, the realm, the given nonce value, the requested URI, and the HTTP method. *generate_md5_key(nonce, username, realm, URI, password_given_by_user)*.

4. The server takes the username, realm, and the requested *URI*, and it looks up the password for the given username. When found, it generates its own version of let's say *generate_md5_key(nonce, username, realm, URI, HTTP method, password-for-this-user-in-my-db)*.

5. The server then compares the output of *generate_md5()* that it got with the one the client sent and

    a. If they match, the client sent the correct password

    b. If they don't match, the password sent was wrong

How to Configure It

web.xml:

```
<login-config>
<auth-method>DIGEST</auth-method>
<realm-name>enterprisesocialdigestrealm</realm-name>
</login-config>
```

Client Authentication

What It Is

An authentication mechanism where the client is securely granted access to a server by exchanging a digital certificate.

You may come across the term "public key certificate" instead of "digital certificate." Both terms are equivalent and serve the same purpose.

How It Works

First of all, it is important to stress that client authentication is a more secure method of authentication than either basic or form-based authentication. Its main advantage is that it uses HTTP over SSL (HTTPS), in which the server authenticates the client using the client's public key certificate.

While client authentication may be fine for intranet applications, it often doesn't scale on the Internet because of the challenge of providing client certificates to thousands of users during their registration and revoking them during their de-registration.

SSL technology provides data encryption, server authentication, message integrity, and optional client authentication for a TCP/IP connection.

The certificate is issued by a certificate authority (CA), which is a trusted organization and provides identification to a bearer.

How to Configure It

Web.xml:

```
<login-config>
<auth-method>CLIENT-CERT</auth-method>
</login-config>
```

Custom Form Authentication

What It Is

Similar to the form-based authentication with the main difference here being in the continuation of the authentication dialog. So instead of posting back to the predefined j_security_check action of the form, the Custom Form authentication mechanism continues the authentication dialog by invoking SecurityContext.authenticate() with the credentials the application collected.

The rest of its concepts are pretty much the same as in form-based authentication, so you can refer back to the latter for the *How It Works* and *Simple Application Walkthrough* parts.

How to Define It

```
@Retention(RUNTIME)
@Target(TYPE)
public @interface CustomFormAuthenticationMechanismDefinition {

    @Nonbinding
    LoginToContinue loginToContinue();
}
```

Identity Stores

In this section, you will get introduced to the concepts of identity stores and their importance to security. Also, you will have a brief look at a basic setup of an identity store in Jakarta EE, which will be extended to an in-depth analysis in the following chapter.

What Is an Identity Store?

An *identity store* is a component that stores application-specific identity information for a set of users, such as usernames, groups, roles, group memberships, permissions, and credentials. Occasionally, it may also be used for storing other information such as GUIDs (caller's globally unique identifiers) or other caller attributes.

To simplify the aforementioned definition, you can think of an identity store as a security-specific DAO (Data Access Object).

What Is the Purpose of an Identity Store?

The purpose of an *identity store* is to validate a caller's identity by accessing a caller's identity attributes. That is, an *identity store* provides access to user information and is required for authentication.

The four most important characteristics of an *identity store* are as follows:

1. Provides access to user information

2. Required for authentication

3. Validates credentials

4. Retrieves group membership

An *identity store* can provide capabilities for authentication, authorization, or both.

Identity Store and Jakarta EE

The broader Jakarta EE ecosystem comprises several APIs to help you govern your web application's authentication (*Jakarta Authentication*), authorization (*Jakarta Authorization*), and security standards. The Jakarta EE API specifies, among others, the IdentityStore interface, providing an abstraction for an identity store.

Implementing IdentityStore enables developers to interact with identity stores to authenticate users (i.e., validate their credentials) and to fetch caller groups.

We consider a good *IdentityStore* implementation that one which operates only on context level and is environment agnostic (will run the same way and will provide the same results regardless of the environment that it's ported and run into). That is, a good *IdentityStore* implementation caters a neat *{credentials in, caller data out}* function.

Let's look at the complete interface (without default behavior, signatures only) and try to better understand it:

```
public interface IdentityStore {
    enum ValidationType { VALIDATE, PROVIDE_GROUPS }

    CredentialValidationResult validate(Credential credential);

    Set<String> getCallerGroups(CredentialValidationResult
    validationResult);

    int priority();

    Set<ValidationType> validationTypes();
}
```

The two most important methods of the *IdentityStore* interface are as follows:

- `validate(Credential)` validates a Credential.

- `getCallerGroups(CredentialValidationResult)` fetches caller information.

IdentityStore implementations can choose to handle either or both of these methods, depending on their capabilities and configuration. They can hint which of these two methods they handle by utilizing the set of values the `validationTypes()` method comes with:

- **VALIDATE** – Indicates that it handles the `validate()` method

- **PROVIDE_GROUPS** – Indicates that it handles the `getCallerGroups()` method

- **VALIDATE** and **PROVIDE_GROUPS** combined – Indicates that it handles both methods

You might feel that declaring capabilities is rather confusing, yet it was a conscious decision to ensure an *IdentityStore*'s configuration and implementation are self-governing. That means that an *IdentityStore* could be configured to support one or the other methods during a particular deployment yet it could be written to support both methods.

Validating Credentials

To determine whether a *Credential* is valid or not, you can use the *validate()* method, which, upon successful validation, returns information about the user identified by the *Credential*. An *IdentityStore* may choose not to implement this method as it's optional.

```
CredentialValidationResult validate(Credential credential);
```

As obvious from the method signature, a validation result is of type CredentialValidationResult, which allows methods to retrieve a validation result's status value and, upon successful validation, the ID of the store that validated the credential, the caller principal, the caller's unique ID in the identity store, and the caller's group memberships (if any).

For successful validation, only the caller principal is required.

So what's under the hood of *CredentialValidationResult*? See the class' overview containing only method signatures:

```
public class CredentialValidationResult {

    public enum Status { NOT_VALIDATED, INVALID, VALID }

    public Status getStatus();

    public String getIdentityStoreId();

    public CallerPrincipal getCallerPrincipal();

    public String getCallerDn();

    public String getCallerUniqueId();

    public Set<String> getCallerGroups();
}
```

To begin with, there are three different status values: NOT_VALIDATED, INVALID, and VALID. What do they mean?

- NOT_VALIDATED – Validation was not attempted, because the *IdentityStore* does not handle the supplied *Credential* type.

- INVALID – Validation failed. The supplied *Credential* was invalid or the corresponding user was not found in the user store.

- VALID – Validation succeeded, and the user is authenticated. The caller principal and group (if any) are available *only* with this result status.

Moving forward to the rest of CredentialValidationResult's methods, the identity store ID, caller DN, and caller unique ID aim to help you implement an *IdentityStore* by cooperating with the validate() and getCallerGroups(). They can be used to ensure that the correct caller groups are returned from getCallerGroups() even in environments where the caller's principal name alone is insufficient to uniquely identify the correct user account.

The Credential interface is a generic interface, capable of representing any kind of token or user credential. An *IdentityStore* implementation can support multiple concrete Credential types, where concrete *Credential* is an implementation of the *Credential* interface that represents a particular type of credential. That is achieved implementing the validate(Credential) method and checking the type of Credential passed as an argument.

The IdentityStore interface provides a default implementation of the validate() method that delegates to a method that can handle the provided *Credential* type, assuming such a method is implemented by the IdentityStore:

```
default CredentialValidationResult validate(Credential credential) {
    try {
        return CredentialValidationResult.class.cast(
            MethodHandles.lookup()
                .bind(this, "validate",
                    methodType(CredentialValidationResult.class,
                                credential.getClass())))
                .invoke(credential));
    } catch (NoSuchMethodException e) {
```

```
       return NOT_VALIDATED_RESULT;
    } catch (Throwable e) {
       throw new IllegalStateException(e);
    }
}
```

validate()delegates to the following method of ExampleIdentityStore if passed a UsernamePasswordCredential:

```
public class ExampleIdentityStore implements IdentityStore {

    public CredentialValidationResult validate(
        UsernamePasswordCredential usernamePasswordCredential) {
        // Implementation ...
        return new CredentialValidationResult(...);
    }
}
```

Retrieving Caller Information

The getCallerGroups() method retrieves the set of groups associated with a validated caller. It's an optional method that an *IdentityStore* may choose not to implement:

```
Set<String> getCallerGroups(CredentialValidationResult validationResult);
```

This supports aggregation of identity stores, where one identity store is used to authenticate users and one or more other stores are used to retrieve additional groups.

In such cases, querying identity stores without validating the caller's credentials against the stores is vital.

Declaring Capabilities

There are still a few methods of the IdentityStore interface that we didn't discuss, methods that an implementation can use to declare its capabilities and ordinal priority:

```
enum ValidationType { VALIDATE, PROVIDE_GROUPS }

Set<ValidationType> DEFAULT_VALIDATION_TYPES = EnumSet.of(VALIDATE,
PROVIDE_GROUPS);
```

```
default int priority() {
    return 100;
}

default Set<ValidationType> validationTypes() {
    return DEFAULT_VALIDATION_TYPES;
}
```

Let's have a closer look at the following:

- `priority()` allows an IdentityStore to be configured with an ordinal number indicating the order in which it should be consulted when multiple *Identity stores* are present. Lower numbers represent higher priority; that is, an `IdentityStore` with a lower priority value is called before an *IdentityStore* with a higher priority.

- `validationTypes()` returns a set of `enum` constants of type `ValidationType`, indicating the purposes for which an IdentityStore should be used:

  - `VALIDATE`, to indicate it handles `validate()`

  - `PROVIDE_GROUPS`, to indicate it handles `getCallerGroups()`

  - Both `VALIDATE` and `PROVIDE_GROUPS`, indicating it handles both methods

An *IdentityStore*'s validation types determine three things:

- Authentication only – Any group data it returns must be ignored.

- Providing groups only – Not used for authentication, but to obtain group data for a caller that was authenticated by a different `IdentityStore`.

- Both authentication and any group data it may return.

How to Validate a User Credential

As we learned earlier, we can use an `HttpAuthenticationMechanism` (or another caller) to authenticate a user. However, the former should not interact directly with an `IdentityStore` but instead invokes the `IdentityStoreHandler` to validate credentials. `IdentityStoreHandler` then invokes `IdentityStore`.

So what is the `IdentityStoreHandler` interface about? It defines a mechanism for invoking on `IdentityStore` to validate a user credential and is considered to be a safer way to authenticate a user.

A default `IdentityStoreHandler` implementation is supplied by the container, but you can write your own custom implementation.

Identity stores usually have a one-to-one relation with a data source such as a relational database, LDAP directory, file system, or another similar resource. Hence, implementations of `IdentityStore` use data source–specific APIs to discover authorization data (roles, permissions, etc.), such as JDBC, File IO, Hibernate/JPA, NoSQL, or any other Data Access mechanism.

OAuth

OAuth is an authorization protocol to delegate rights for an application to act on behalf of a user who granted their rights without giving away login credentials like username or password.

It was developed by Twitter, Magnolia, and Google and registered as IETF standard in April 2010 under RFC 5849.

OAuth version 2.0 is simpler to use but often criticized for having too many flavors and implementations. OAuth 2 was standardized again by IETF in October 2012 under RFC 6749 and 6750. It is not backward compatible with OAuth 1.0a.

Some notable adopters are Facebook, Amazon, Google, Salesforce.com, or Microsoft. All relevant social media APIs are based on either OAuth 1.0a or 2.0.

Figure 4-3 shows the actors of the OAuth flow, often also called the "OAuth Dance."

- Resource Owner

- Client

- Server

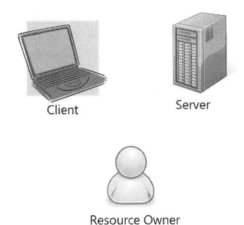

Figure 4-3. *OAuth Parties*

To use OAuth, one has to create an application on the target service to have an entry point for the consumer or resource owner, allowing access tokens to be issued to third-party clients by an authorization server, with the approval of the resource owner, or end user. The client then uses the access token to access the protected resources hosted by the resource server.

The OAuth "Dance" has three major steps:

- Creation – Creating an application in the OAuth Social Media service.

- Initialization – The right granting phase also called the OAuth Dance. At the end of the dance, we obtain an access token (formed by a public and secret part) used in the next step.

- Signature – Each request is signed with access token and token identifying the OAuth application that was granted the rights.

Figure 4-4 shows the steps and authentication flow in detail for OAuth 1.0a.

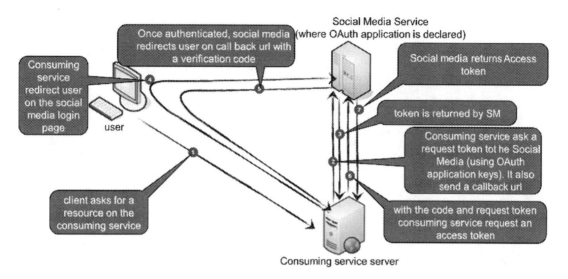

Figure 4-4. *OAuth 1.0a "Dance"*

Figure 4-5 shows the same flow for OAuth 2. You can see the communication has been simplified, plus all exchanges must now be SSL encrypted. With OAuth 1.0a, this was optional, and most implementing cases therefore left it out, bearing a greater risk of interception or tampering than OAuth 2.

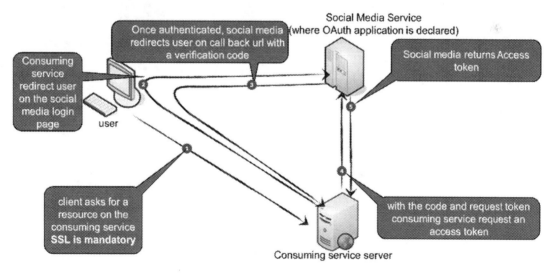

Figure 4-5. *OAuth 2 "Dance"*

While by far the most popular access control for social media and APIs, OAuth is not a genuine authentication, but "pseudo-authentication," where the application specifically requests a limited access OAuth Token ("valet key") rather than actual credentials (like a "passport"); see Figures 4-6 and 4-7.

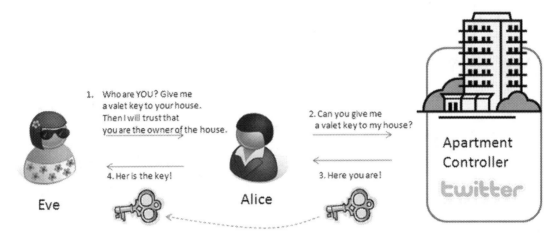

Figure 4-6. *Pseudo-authentication Using OAuth*

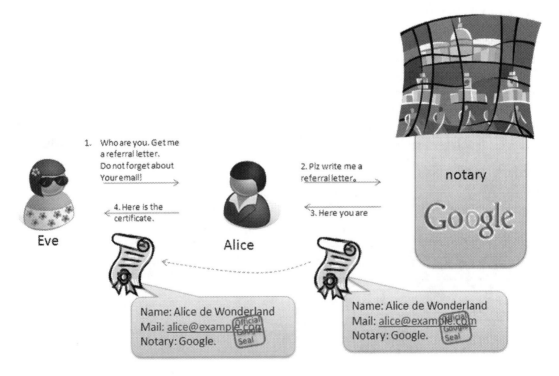

Figure 4-7. *OpenID Authentication*

OpenID

The initial OpenID protocol was created in 2005 by Brad Fitzpatrick at Six Apart, after he had sold his social network LiveJournal to this blog software company. The name of the company did not refer to Six Degrees of Separation [6] as it may seem, but a six-day age difference between its married co-founders.

It was code-named Yadis (acronym for "Yet another distributed identity system") but was then officially called OpenID after David Lehn, who had also considered a similar Single Sign-On project but lacked time and donated the domain "openid.net" [29] to Six Apart.

Figure 4-8 shows the OpenID flow and its actors:

- Browser

- User

- Relying party

- Identity provider

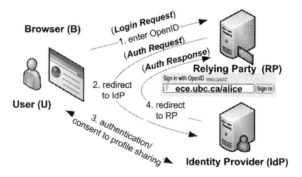

Figure 4-8. *OpenID Flow*

While OpenID had not been standardized by an organization like IETF, many large Internet, social media, and Telco players applied it, like AOL, Blogger, Flickr, France Telecom, Google, Hyves, LiveJournal, Microsoft, Mixi, Myspace, Novell, Orange, Sears, Sun, Telecom Italia, Telefonica O2, Universal Music Group, Verisign, WordPress, or Yahoo!

Over time others like SourceForge, PayPal, or Facebook joined supporters of OpenID under the OpenID Foundation. However, in the last two to three years, there's been a steady decline in OpenID supporters. Facebook left OpenID, SourceForge also stopped offering an OpenID login (at the very least after Dice.com took it over from Geeknet), and in September 2013, Social Login SaaS provider Janrain announced that its service MyOpenID.com would be shut down on February 1, 2014.

So did that mean OpenID was dead? More or less in its original form, but at least still Google has high hopes for it. Strange coincidence, the initial creator of OpenID, Brad Fitzpatrick, now works at Google, probably a main reason why the company remained loyal to OpenID, when most other former supporters abandoned it. OpenID Connect, Google's new approach, has, however, not that much in common with the old version of OpenID. It adds improved authentication and Identity Management on top of the otherwise winning combination of OAuth 2, JSON, and RESTful Web Services.

OpenID Connect

OpenID Connect was released by the OpenID Foundation at the end of February 2014. Besides Google, Microsoft, Salesforce.com, or Deutsche Telekom adopted it at the time. At Mobile World Congress 2014 in Barcelona, GSMA announced plans for a mobile version "Mobile Connect," enough suggesting it would stay for some time.

OpenID Connect is extensible, supporting optional features like encrypting identity data, discovery of OpenID providers, or session management.

JWT

JSON Web Token (JWT) is an open standard filed under RFC 7519 to securely transmit information between different applications or services via JSON strings.

JWT is compact, human-readable, and digitally signed using a private or public key pair identity provider (IdP). So the integrity and authenticity of the token can be verified by other involved parties.

The main purpose of JWT is not to hide data but to ensure its authenticity. JWT is mainly used to sign and encode, but not encrypt data, although the tokens may also be encrypted based on another set of standards including JSON Web Signature (JWS) and JSON Web Encryption (JWE).

JWT is a token-based stateless authentication mechanism. Since it is based on a client-side stateless session, servers don't need a persistence mechanism like a database to save information about the session. JSON Web Tokens follow a well-defined and known standard that is becoming the most common token format to protect services.

Use Cases

Two of the main use cases for JSON Web Token are as follows:

- Authorization

- Information Exchange

Authorization is probably the most common use case for JWT. Once the user has logged into a system, each subsequent request will include the JWT, allowing the user to access pages, services, and resources that are permitted by that token. Single Sign-On is a feature that widely uses JWT nowadays, especially in public APIs, because of its small overhead and ability to be easily used across different domains.

Information Exchange: JSON Web Tokens are a good way of securely transmitting information between parties. Because JWTs can be signed – for example, using public/ private key pairs – you can be sure the senders are who they say they are. Additionally, as the signature is calculated using the header and the payload, you can also verify that the content has not been tampered with.

Why Do We Need JWT?

The HTTP protocol is stateless; therefore, a new request such as GET /order/42 doesn't know anything about the previous ones like PUT /order with the same id, and a user would have to authenticate again for every new request.

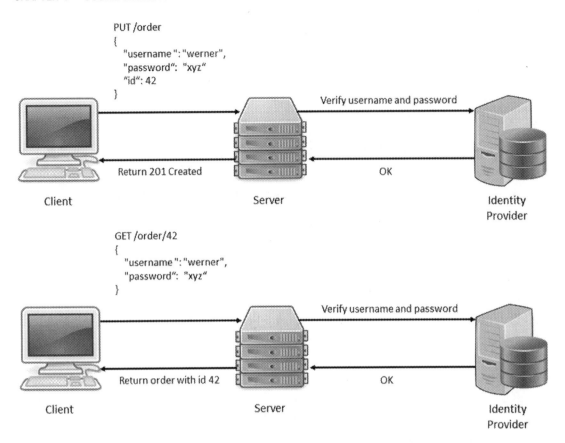

Figure 4-9. *Repeating Authentication for Every New HTTP API Request*

This is often dealt with by using Server-Side Sessions (SSS). First, the login credentials are like username and password are checked, and if they are correct, the server will create a session id, store it, and return it to the client. In Jakarta EE applications based on Servlets, this cookie sent to the client is usually called JSESSIONID.

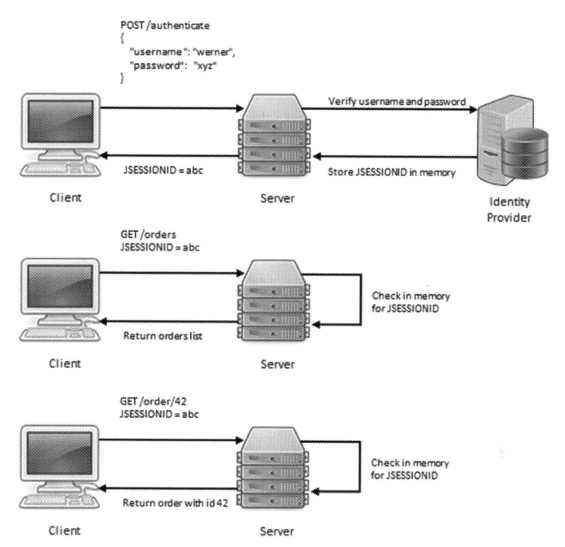

Figure 4-10. *Using SSS, Reducing the Number of Authentications Against the Identity Provider*

This approach can fix one problem but may create others like scalability issues. While Server-Side Sessions may work well for most websites and even a few e-commerce shops, in an API-driven era, some endpoints can face a massive number of requests forcing the provider to scale. There are two ways to scale:

- Vertical scaling

- Horizontal scaling

Vertical scaling means adding more resources like memory, storage, or CPU cores to a server. This can be quite expensive and also reach certain limits, for example, the number of CPUs, memory slots, or disk storage per server.

Horizontal scaling scales out your infrastructure by adding more servers behind a **load balancer**, which is usually more efficient and cost-effective than upgrading each of the servers all the time. While scaling horizontally is usually more efficient, it leads to further problems and complexity even with just one location and load balancer.

Imagine a single server behind a load balancer and a client performing a request using a JSESSIONID like **"abc"**; that session id can be found in the server's memory.

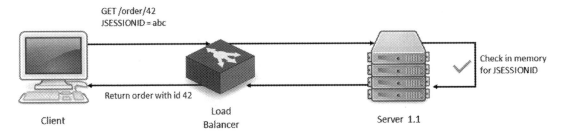

Figure 4-11. *Single Server Behind a Load Balancer*

If the infrastructure needs to scale and a new server is added behind the load balancer this new server gets to handle the next request by a client using **"abc"**, it will not recognize that JSESSIONID.

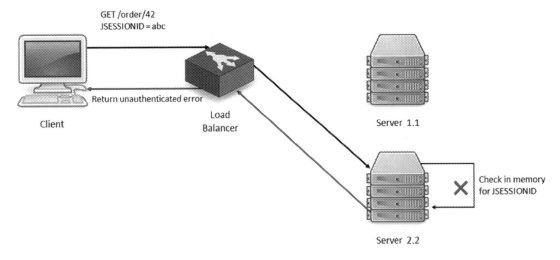

Figure 4-12. *New Server Behind LB, User Not Recognized*

Authentication fails because the new server has no **"abc"** sessions in its memory yet. There are three main workarounds to address this.

Synchronize the sessions between servers, which can be tricky and error-prone, especially in a globally distributed architecture.

Use an external database or session caching mechanism. This can be helpful but adds more components to the infrastructure, and especially in a distributed environment, this cache or DB will need its own replication.

Or accept the stateless nature of HTTP and try to find a solution that works for it.

That's where JSON Web Token comes to the rescue, because each token is compact and self-contained, so it contains all the necessary information to allow or deny an API request without having to perform any replication or costly lookups first.

How Does It Work?

Token-based authentication mechanisms allow systems to authenticate, authorize, and verify identities based on a security token. Usually, the following entities are involved:

- Issuer – Responsible for issuing security tokens as a result of successfully asserting an identity (authentication). Issuers are usually related with identity providers.

- Client – Represented by an application to which the token was issued for. Clients are usually related to service providers. A client may also act as an intermediary between a subject and a target service (delegation).

- Subject – The entity to which the information in a token refers to.

- Resource server – Represented by an application that is going to consume the token in order to check if it grants access or not to a protected resource.

Independent of the token format or applied protocol, from a service perspective, token-based authentication is comprised of the following steps:

1. Extract security token from the request.

   For RESTful services, this is usually achieved by obtaining the token from the Authorization header.

2. Perform validation checks against the token.

   This step usually depends on the token format and security protocol in use. The objective is to make sure the token is valid and can be consumed by the application. It may involve signature, encryption, and expiration checks.

3. Introspect the token and extract information about the subject.

   This step usually depends on the token format and security protocol in use. The objective is to obtain all the necessary information about the subject from the token.

4. Create a security context for the subject.

Based on the information extracted from the token, the application creates a security context for the subject in order to use the information wherever necessary when serving protected resources.

JWT Structure

A JSON Web Token has three parts:

- Header
- Payload
- Signature

Each of these parts is separated by a "." character.
Therefore, every JWT looks like

```
Header.Payload.Signature
```

Header

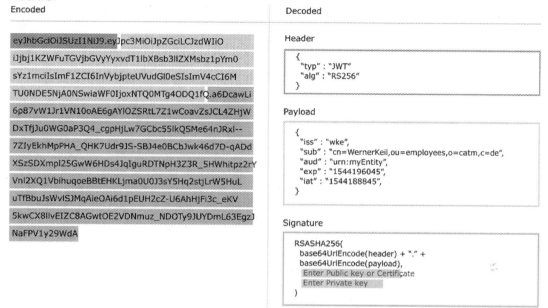

Figure 4-13. JWT Structure

The header describes the JSON Web Token itself. It contains the information about the type of the token and the algorithm used to generate the signature. The algorithm parameter **"alg"** must be present in every JWT header. The most common algorithms are HMAC with a SHA-256 hash ("HS256") or RSA with the same ("RS256") and more recently ECDSA P-256 with SHA-256 ("ES256"). The allowed values are specified by the JSON Web Encryption (JWE) standard RFC 7516.

In our example, the header contains the algorithm and type parameters:

```
{
    "typ" : "JWT",
    "alg" : "RS256"
}
```

The type parameter **"typ"** is used to declare the IANA media type (RFC 6838) of the token. It is optional, but when set, it should always be "JWT", representing the media type `"application/jwt"`.

Another parameter **"cty"** (content type) is used to declare the media type of the secured content (payload). It is optional and only required if the payload contains another JSON Web Token, in which case its value should be "JWT"; otherwise, this parameter can be ignored or left out.

The parameter **"enc"** (encryption algorithm) is defined for use with JWE. It is only required when the claims or nested JWT tokens have to be encrypted. It identifies the cryptographic algorithm used to encrypt the claims or nested JWT tokens.

For example, AES in the Galois/Counter Mode (GCM) algorithm using a 256-bit key would be specified as "A256GCM".

There are several other predefined header parameters like

- crit (Critical)

- jku (JWK Set URL)

- jwk (JSON Web Key)

- kid (Key ID)

- x5u (X.509 URL)

- x5t (X.509 Certificate SHA-1 Thumbprint)

- x5t#S256 (X.509 Certificate SHA-256 Thumbprint)

Payload

The payload or body is the essential part of the JWT containing security statements like the identity of the user and granted permissions. JWT calls them claims.

There are three types of JWT claim names:

1. Registered claim

2. Public claim

3. Private claim

Registered claims are the predefined claims. Public claims can be any user-defined information, and private claims are those upon which the producer and consumer of JWT agreed to use in a specific application.

In order to validate a JWT, we should check some registered claims as well. Some important registered claims are defined in Table 4-1.

Table 4-1. *Registered JWT Claims*

Claim Name	Description	Reference
iss	The token issuer	RFC 7519, Section 4.1.1
sub	The principal that is the subject of the JWT	RFC 7519, Section 4.1.2
aud	The recipients of the JWT	RFC 7519, Section 4.1.3
exp	The expiration time on or after which the JWT must not be accepted for processing	RFC 7519, Section 4.1.4
nbf	Time before which the JWT must not be accepted for processing	RFC 7519, Section 4.1.5
iat	Time at which the issuer generated the JWT	RFC 7519, Section 4.1.6
jti	Unique identifier for the JWT	RFC 7519, Section 4.1.7

"iss" (Issuer) Claim

The "iss" (issuer) claim identifies the principal that issued the JWT. The processing of this claim is generally application specific. The "iss" value is a case-sensitive string containing a URI value. The use of this claim is optional. We should validate that the issuer is a valid URL or the JWT was sent by an expected issuer.

"sub" (Subject) Claim

The "sub" (subject) claim identifies the principal that is the subject of the token. Claims in a JWT are statements about the subject. The "sub" value is a case-sensitive string containing a URI value. The use of this claim is optional.

"aud" (Audience) Claim

The "aud" (audience) claim identifies the recipients of the token. Each principal intended to process the JWT must identify itself with a value in the audience claim. If the principal processing the claim does not identify itself with a value in the "aud" claim when this claim is present, then the JWT must be rejected. In general, the "aud" value is an array of case-sensitive strings, each containing a URI value. The use of this claim is optional.

"exp" (Expiration Time) Claim

The "exp" (expiration time) claim identifies the expiration time on or after which the token will not be accepted for processing. The processing of the "exp" claim requires that the current date/time must be before the expiration date/time listed in the "exp" claim. Its value must be a numeric timestamp. The use of this claim is optional.

"nbf" (Not Before) Claim

The "nbf" (not before) claim identifies the time before which the JWT must not be accepted for processing. The processing of the "nbf" claim requires that the current date/time must be after or equal to the not-before date/time listed in the "nbf" claim. Its value must be a number containing a numeric date value. This claim is optional.

"iat" (Issued At) Claim

The "iat" (issued at) claim identifies the time at which the token was issued. This claim can be used to determine the age of the JWT. Its value must be a number containing a numeric date value. This claim is optional.

"jti" (JWT ID) Claim

The "jti" (JWT ID) claim provides a case-sensitive unique identifier for the JWT. The identifier value must be assigned in a manner that ensures that there is a negligible probability that the same value will be accidentally assigned to a different data object; if the application uses multiple issuers, collisions must be prevented among values produced by different issuers as well. The "jti" claim can be used to prevent the JWT from being reused. The use of this claim is optional.

Signature

The third part of the JSON Web Token is the signature. It is the most important part of a JWT to validate it and ensure it was not modified or tampered with and can be trusted. The signature is generated using the payload and a secret key; therefore, anyone in possession of this key can generate new tokens with valid signatures.

The most commonly used cryptographic algorithms to generate a signature are as follows:

- HS256, which is short for HMAC-SHA256

- RS256, short for RSA-SHA256

- ES256, short for ECDSA P-256 SHA-256

HS256 is a symmetric key encryption and involves a secret key being shared between two parties. This secret key is used to encrypt the data, and on the receiver side, the same key is used to decrypt the data. HS256 signatures are generated using a secret key that is validated at the receiving end (resource server). On the receiver side, using the payload and secret key, the signature has to be generated again and compared to the signature part of the incoming JWT. Since only the authentication server and resource server are in possession of the secret key, it is not possible to tamper with the JWT, and we can ensure its validity.

MicroProfile JWT

A frustrating aspect of many standards is that some aim to be a jack of all trades offering a massive number of choices. This is definitely the case with JWT, which allows multiple types of digital signatures and many possible claims. While the possibilities are infinite, so many options mean infinite opportunities for interoperability issues.

A critical goal of MicroProfile JWT is to take just enough of these options that the basic interoperability across enterprises can be achieved in a way that favors microservices in particular.

The focus of the MicroProfile JWT specification is the definition of the required format of JWT usable for interoperable authentication and authorization. MP JWT also maps JWT claims to various Jakarta EE container APIs and makes the set of claims available through getter methods.

The sources for the specification, API, and TCK are available from the Eclipse microprofile-jwt-auth GitHub repository.

The purpose of MP JWT as a token format depends on the agreement between identity providers and service providers. This means identity providers – responsible for issuing tokens – should be able to issue interoperable tokens using the MP JWT format in a way that service providers can understand in order to validate the token and gather information about a subject. With that respect, requirements for the MicroProfile JWT are as follows:

1. Be usable as an authentication token

2. Be usable as an authorization token that contains Jakarta EE application–level roles indirectly granted via a `groups` claim

3. Able to support additional standard claims described in IANA JWT specification as well as nonstandard claims

To meet those requirements, MP JWT introduced two new claims:

- "upn" – A human-readable claim that uniquely identifies the subject or user principal of the token, across MicroProfile services accessing the token

- "groups" – The token subject's group memberships that will be mapped to Java EE style application–level roles in the MicroProfile service container

The specification (as of 2.1) is based on the following Jakarta EE API dependencies:

- Jakarta RESTful Web Services 3.0

- Jakarta JSON Processing 2.0

- Jakarta JSON Binding 2.0

- CDI 3.0

- Jakarta Annotations 2.0

The MicroProfile JWT specification is focused on the ability of microservices to verify JWTs and does not define the following:

- JWT creation – Tokens will typically be created by a dedicated service in the enterprise like an API gateway or an identity provider.

- RSA public key distribution – Distributing the public key of the gateway or identity provider is out of scope for MP JWT. Like TLS/SSL certificates, they may not change often, and distributing them manually or installing them, for example, docker images, is a common practice.

- Automatic JWT propagation – Microservices using MP JWT have a guaranteed and standard way to obtain the JWT on incoming calls. However, propagation must be done by the microservice itself in the application code by placing the JWT in the Authorization header of outgoing HTTP calls.

It is a critical goal of MicroProfile JWT that the token can be both verified and propagated by each microservice. For reasons discussed in the trouble with HS256, MicroProfile JWT chooses RSA-based digital signatures only.

The RSA public key of the authorization server, which creates the JWTs, can be installed on all the microservices in advance of any actual HTTP requests. When calls come into a microservice, it will use this RSA public key to verify the JWT and determine if the caller's identity is valid. If any HTTP calls are made by the microservice, it should pass the JWT in those calls, propagating the caller's identity forward to other microservices.

As defined by the JWT standard, the **"alg"** header parameter must be present. If claims or nested JWT tokens are encrypted, **"enc"** is also a mandatory header parameter.

The use of the header parameters **"typ"** and **"kid"** is recommended.

While the JWT specification declares pretty much every registered claim as optional, MicroProfile JWT requires the following claims to be present:

- iss

- iat

- exp

The use of these JWT claims is recommended by MP JWT:

- sub

- jti

- aud

In addition to the registered JWT claims listed in Table 4-1, MicroProfile JWT defines the public claims of its own (Table 4-2).

Table 4-2. *MP JWT Public Claims*

Claim Name	Description	Reference
upn	Provides the user principal name in the `java.security.Principal` interface. This claim is required	MP-JWT 2.1 specification
groups	Provides the list of group names that have been assigned to the principal of the MP-JWT. This typically will require a mapping at the application container level to application deployment roles, but a one-to-one between group names and application role names is required to be performed in addition to any other mapping. This claim is optional	MP-JWT 2.1 specification

It is recommended that JWT tokens have a **"groups"** claim if the endpoint requires authorization, but MP JWT implementations can map the groups from other claims if the tokens have been issued by OpenID Connect and other providers that currently do not support MP JWT.

If no groups information can be extracted directly from the **"groups"** claim or via custom mappers from other claims in a given token, then this token can be accepted if the endpoint requires authentication only.

Numeric date values used by **"exp"**, **"iat"**, and other date-related claims are a JSON numeric value representing the number of **seconds** from `1970-01-01T00:00:00Z UTC` until the specified UTC date/time, ignoring leap seconds.

MicroProfile JWT implementations may enforce that JWT tokens contain all the recommended headers and claims. The recommended headers and claims may become required in the future versions of the MP JWT specification.

An example minimal MP JWT in JSON would be

```
{
    "typ": "JWT",
    "alg": "RS256",
    "kid": "abc-1234567890"
}
```

```
{
    "iss": "https://server.example.com",
    "jti": "a-123",
    "exp": 1311281970,
    "iat": 1311280970,
    "sub": "24400320",
    "upn": "jdoe@server.example.com",
    "groups": ["red-group", "green-group", "admin-group"],
}
```

The MicroProfile JWT specification defines a **JsonWebToken** java.security. Principal interface extension that makes this set of required claims available via get methods.

Summary

After standardization of social media interaction and APIs, this chapter showed us the security aspects of social networks and standards aiming at security. In the following chapter, we'll discover security frameworks that make use of or implement some of these standards.

CHAPTER 5

Security Frameworks

The previous chapter dealt with security aspects of social networks and standards related to security. In this chapter, we'll cover security frameworks like Soteria, Keycloak, Spring Security, Micronaut Security, Apache Shiro, or Scribe, supporting authorization, authentication, or both.

Soteria

Eclipse Soteria is the compatible implementation of Jakarta Security.

The word "Soteria" is Greek and means "rescue," "wellbeing," or "salvation".

History

The term "Soteria" was picked in a survey conducted by Werner Keil among EG members while Soteria was the RI of JSR 375, then started as Java EE Security.

Especially in Europe it is also used in a healthcare context, often related to clinics for psychological problems, but that was a pure coincidence. After the transition to Jakarta EE at the Eclipse Foundation, the legal team checked all trademarks for the term that might exist and had no concerns, while other projects, especially "Ozark" (the MVC compatible implementation), had to be renamed to "Krazo."

Authentication Mechanisms

The foundation of the authentication mechanism implementation is `HttpAuthenticationMechanism`, which makes the respective mechanism available as a CDI bean. The implemented method `validateRequest()` returns an `AuthenticationStatus` object containing the status of that authentication. The specification provides out-of-the-box mechanisms for basic authentication and form-based authentication.

© Werner Keil 2024
W. Keil, *Enterprise Social for the Java Platform*, https://doi.org/10.1007/978-1-4842-9571-7_5

The Jakarta Servlet specification defines a declarative mechanism for configuring an application to provide **BASIC**, **DIGEST**, **FORM**, or **CERT** authentication, with authentication performed automatically by the container based on the application's configuration, FORM authentication, can include custom form pages.

In addition, a Jakarta EE *container must* support built-in beans for the following HttpAuthenticationMechanism types, made available via configuration:

- BASIC – Uses the standard Basic Authentication Scheme described in RFC 2617. There is no encryption of credentials unless you use SSL. This type is not a secure method unless used with SSL. This bean is activated and configured via the @ BasicAuthenticationMechanismDefinition annotation.

- FORM – The application provides its own custom login and error pages. The communication protocol is HTTP with optional SSL. There is no encryption of user credentials unless SSL is used. This bean is activated and configured via the @ FormAuthenticationMechanismDefinition annotation.

- Custom FORM – A variant on FORM, with the difference that continuing the authentication dialog as described in the Servlet spec does not happen by posting back to j_security_check, but by invoking SecurityContext.authenticate() with the credentials collected by the application. This bean is activated and configured via the @CustomFormAuthenticationMechanismDefinition annotation.

- OpenID Connect – Authenticates according to the Authorization Code flow and Refresh tokens as defined by the OpenID Connect specification [29]. This bean is activated and configured via the @ OpenIdAuthenticationMechanismDefinition annotation.

Jakarta Security has versions of Basic and Form that *must* match the Servlet spec, but GlassFish doesn't use them in web applications when defined in the web.xml, only when defined via annotations.

Here's an example for the BasicAuthenticationMechanism in Soteria:

```
package org.glassfish.soteria.mechanisms;

import static java.lang.String.format;
```

```
import static jakarta.security.enterprise.identitystore.
CredentialValidationResult.Status.VALID;
import static jakarta.xml.bind.DatatypeConverter.parseBase64Binary;
import static org.glassfish.soteria.Utils.isEmpty;

import jakarta.security.enterprise.AuthenticationException;
import jakarta.security.enterprise.AuthenticationStatus;
import jakarta.security.enterprise.authentication.mechanism.http.
BasicAuthenticationMechanismDefinition;
import jakarta.security.enterprise.authentication.mechanism.http.
HttpAuthenticationMechanism;
import jakarta.security.enterprise.authentication.mechanism.http.
HttpMessageContext;
import jakarta.security.enterprise.credential.Password;
import jakarta.security.enterprise.credential.UsernamePasswordCredential;
import jakarta.security.enterprise.identitystore.
CredentialValidationResult;
import jakarta.security.enterprise.identitystore.IdentityStoreHandler;
import jakarta.servlet.http.HttpServletRequest;
import jakarta.servlet.http.HttpServletResponse;

import org.glassfish.soteria.cdi.CdiUtils;

/**
 * Authentication mechanism that authenticates using basic authentication
 *
 * @author Arjan Tijms
 *
 */
public class BasicAuthenticationMechanism implements
HttpAuthenticationMechanism {

    private final BasicAuthenticationMechanismDefinition
    basicAuthenticationMechanismDefinition;

    // CDI requires a no-arg constructor to be portable
    // It's only used to create the proxy
    protected BasicAuthenticationMechanism() {
```

```
            basicAuthenticationMechanismDefinition = null;
    }

    public BasicAuthenticationMechanism(BasicAuthentication
    MechanismDefinition basicAuthenticationMechanismDefinition) {
            this.basicAuthenticationMechanismDefinition =
            basicAuthenticationMechanismDefinition;
    }

        @Override
        public AuthenticationStatus validateRequest(HttpServletReque
        st request, HttpServletResponse response, HttpMessageContext
        httpMsgContext) throws AuthenticationException {

                String[] credentials = getCredentials(request);
                if (!isEmpty(credentials)) {

                IdentityStoreHandler identityStoreHandler = CdiUtils.getBeanRef
                erence(IdentityStoreHandler.class);

                CredentialValidationResult result = identityStoreHandler.
                validate(
                        new UsernamePasswordCredential(credentials[0], new
                        Password(credentials[1])));

                if (result.getStatus() == VALID) {
                    return httpMsgContext.notifyContainerAboutLogin(
                        result.getCallerPrincipal(), result.getCallerGroups());
                    }
                }

                if (httpMsgContext.isProtected()) {
                        response.setHeader("WWW-Authenticate", format("Basic
                        realm=\"%s\"", basicAuthenticationMechanismDefinition.
                        realmName()));
                        return httpMsgContext.responseUnauthorized();
                }

                return httpMsgContext.doNothing();
```

```
    }

    private String[] getCredentials(HttpServletRequest request) {

        String authorizationHeader = request.
        getHeader("Authorization");
        if (!isEmpty(authorizationHeader) && authorizationHeader.
        startsWith("Basic ") ) {
            return new String(parseBase64Binary(authorizationHeader.
            substring(6))).split(":");
        }
        return null;
    }

}
```

Supported Runtimes

Soteria runs on the following Jakarta EE CI runtimes:

- GlassFish

- Payara

- WildFly

- Open Liberty

In addition, all implementations that use Soteria under "Implementation Components" run or contain it.

With some adjustments, it also runs on TomEE, but since TomEE 9+ and Open Liberty come with their own implementations of Jakarta Security (not based on Soteria), those can be a little more complicated.

OpenID Connect Example

Let's see how to configure OpenID Connect authentication in a Jakarta EE web application with OpenID Connect authentication providers like a local Keycloak instance or social networks like Google.

First, we create a simple web project, for example, by using the Maven Webapp Archetype:

```
mvn archetype:generate
    -DarchetypeGroupId=org.apache.maven.archetypes
    -DarchetypeArtifactId=maven-archetype-webapp
    -DarchetypeVersion=1.4
```

Then we update the POM:

```
<project xmlns="http://maven.apache.org/POM/4.0.0" xmlns:xsi="http://www.
w3.org/2001/XMLSchema-instance"
        xsi:schemaLocation="http://maven.apache.org/POM/4.0.0
        http://maven.apache.org/xsd/maven-4.0.0.xsd">
    <modelVersion>4.0.0</modelVersion>
    <groupId>com.demo</groupId>
    <artifactId>jakarta-ee-oidc-example</artifactId>
    <version>1.0-SNAPSHOT</version>
    <packaging>war</packaging>

    <name>Jakarta EE 10 OIDC Example</name>
    <description>Example Jakarta EE OIDC application</description>
    <properties>          <project.build.sourceEncoding>UTF-8</project.build.
    sourceEncoding>          <project.reporting.outputEncoding>UTF-8
    </project.reporting.outputEncoding>
        <maven.compiler.release>17</maven.compiler.release>
        <!-- Maven Plugins -->          <maven-compiler-plugin.
        version>3.10.1</maven-compiler-plugin.version>
        <maven-war-plugin.version>3.3.2</maven-war-plugin.version>
        <maven-dependency-plugin.version>3.3.0</maven-dependency-plugin.
        version>          <maven-surefire-plugin.version>3.0.0-M7
        </maven-surefire-plugin.version>          <maven-failsafe-plugin.
        version>3.0.0-M7</maven-failsafe-plugin.version>
        <maven-surefire-report-plugin.version>3.0.0-M7</maven-surefire-
        report-plugin.version>
        <!-- Jakarta EE API -->
        <jakartaee-api.version>10.0.0</jakartaee-api.version>
```

```
    <!-- by default skip tests -->
    <skip.unit.tests>false</skip.unit.tests>
    <skip.integration.tests>true</skip.integration.tests>

    <!-- Wildfly server -->
    <wildfly.artifactId>wildfly-dist</wildfly.artifactId>
    <wildfly.version>27.0.1.Final</wildfly.version>
    <wildfly-maven-plugin.version>4.0.0.Final</wildfly-maven-plugin.
    version>          <jboss-as.home>${project.build.directory}/wildfly-
    ${wildfly.version}</jboss-as.home>
</properties>
<dependencies>
    <dependency>
        <groupId>jakarta.platform</groupId>
        <artifactId>jakarta.jakartaee-api</artifactId>
        <version>${jakartaee-api.version}</version>
        <scope>provided</scope>
    </dependency>
</dependencies>
<build>
    <finalName>${project.artifactId}</finalName>
    <pluginManagement>
        <plugins>
            <plugin>
                <groupId>org.codehaus.cargo</groupId>
                <artifactId>cargo-maven3-plugin</artifactId>
                <version>${cargo-maven3-plugin.version}</version>
            </plugin>
        </plugins>
    </pluginManagement>
    <plugins>
        <plugin>
            <groupId>org.apache.maven.plugins</groupId>
            <artifactId>maven-compiler-plugin</artifactId>
            <version>${maven-compiler-plugin.version}</version>
        </plugin>
```

```
<plugin>
    <groupId>org.apache.maven.plugins</groupId>
    <artifactId>maven-war-plugin</artifactId>
    <version>${maven-war-plugin.version}</version>
</plugin>
<plugin>
    <groupId>org.apache.maven.plugins</groupId>
    <artifactId>maven-surefire-plugin</artifactId>
    <version>${maven-surefire-plugin.version}</version>
    <configuration>
        <skipTests>${skip.unit.tests}</skipTests>
    </configuration>
    <executions>
        <execution>
            <id>default-test</id>
            <phase>test</phase>
            <goals>
                <goal>test</goal>
            </goals>
            <configuration>
                <excludes>
                    <exclude>**/it/**</exclude>
                </excludes>
            </configuration>
        </execution>
    </executions>
</plugin>
<plugin>
    <groupId>org.apache.maven.plugins</groupId>
    <artifactId>maven-failsafe-plugin</artifactId>
      <version>${maven-failsafe-plugin.version}</version>
    <configuration>
        <skipITs>${skip.integration.tests}</skipITs>
    </configuration>
    <executions>
```

```
    <execution>
        <id>integration-test</id>
        <phase>integration-test</phase>
        <goals>
            <goal>integration-test</goal>
            <goal>verify</goal>
        </goals>
        <configuration>
            <includes>
                <include>**/it/**</include>
            </includes>
        </configuration>
    </execution>
</executions>
</plugin>
<plugin>
    <groupId>org.apache.maven.plugins</groupId>
    <artifactId>maven-dependency-plugin</artifactId>
    <version>${maven-dependency-plugin.version}</version>
    <executions>
        <execution>
            <id>unpack</id>
            <phase>process-classes</phase>
            <goals>
                <goal>unpack</goal>
            </goals>
            <configuration>
                <artifactItems>
                    <artifactItem>
                        <groupId>org.wildfly</groupId>
                        <artifactId>${wildfly.artifactId}
                        </artifactId>
                        <version>${wildfly.version}</version>
```

```xml
<type>zip</type>
                                            <overWrite>false
                                            </overWrite>
                            <outputDirectory>${project.build.
                            directory}</outputDirectory>
                    </artifactItem>
                </artifactItems>
            </configuration>
        </execution>
    </executions>
</plugin>
<plugin>
    <groupId>org.wildfly.plugins</groupId>
    <artifactId>wildfly-maven-plugin</artifactId>
    <version>${wildfly-maven-plugin.version}</version>
    <configuration>
        <commands>
            <command>/subsystem=undertow/application-security-
            domain=other:write-attribute(name=integrated-jaspi,
            value=false)</command>
            <command>reload</command>
        </commands>
    </configuration>
</plugin>
        </plugins>
    </build>
</project>
```

The example is configured for WildFly 27 or higher, but it would equally work on any of the Supported Runtimes.

Next we create a CDI bean for the OIDC authentication:

```java
@OpenIdAuthenticationMechanismDefinition(
        clientId = "${oidcConfig.clientId}",
        clientSecret = "${oidcConfig.clientSecret}",
        redirectURI = "${baseURL}/callback",
```

```
        providerURI = "${oidcConfig.issuerUri}",
        jwksConnectTimeout = 5000,
        jwksReadTimeout = 5000
        )
@ApplicationScoped
@Named("oidcConfig")
public class OidcConfig {
private static final Logger LOGGER = Logger.getLogger(OidcConfig.class.
getName());
private String domain;
private String clientId;
private String clientSecret;
private String issuerUri;
@PostConstruct
void init() {
      LOGGER.config("OidcConfig.init()");
try {
var properties = new Properties();
properties.load(getClass().getResourceAsStream("/oidc.properties"));
domain = properties.getProperty("domain");
clientId = properties.getProperty("clientId");
clientSecret = properties.getProperty("clientSecret");
issuerUri = properties.getProperty("issuerUri");
if (issuerUri == null && domain != null) {
issuerUri = ("localhost".equals(this.domain) ? "http://" : "https://") +
this.domain + "/";
}
LOGGER.log(
Level.INFO,
"domain: {0}, clientId: {1}, clientSecret:{2}, issuerUri: {3}",
new Object[] {
domain,
clientId,
clientSecret,
issuerUri
```

```
});
} catch (IOException e) {
LOGGER.log(Level.SEVERE, "Failed to load oidc.properties", e);
}
}
public String getDomain() {
return domain;
}
public String getClientId() {
return clientId;
}
public String getClientSecret() {
return clientSecret;
}
public String getIssuerUri() {
return issuerUri;
}
}
```

The PublicServlet is a simple, unsecured servlet:

```
@WebServlet("/public")
public class PublicServlet extends HttpServlet {
    @Override
    protected void doGet(HttpServletRequest request, HttpServletResponse
    response) throws IOException, IOException {
        response.setContentType("text/html");
        response.getWriter().println("<h1>Public Unsecured Servlet</h1>");
    }
}
```

The ProtectedServlet is secured, and we also declare roles for this application. foo is allowed to access this servlet:

```
@WebServlet("/protected")
@DeclareRoles({"foo", "bar", "kaz"})
@ServletSecurity(
        @HttpConstraint(rolesAllowed = "foo")
```

```
)
public class ProtectedServlet extends HttpServlet {
    @Inject
    private OpenIdContext context;
    @Override
    protected void doGet(HttpServletRequest request, HttpServletResponse
    response) throws IOException {
        response.setContentType("text/html");
        response.getWriter().println("<h1>Protected Servlet</h1>");
        response.getWriter().println("<p>access token:" + context.
        getAccessToken() + "</p>");
        response.getWriter().println("<p>token type:" + context.
        getTokenType() + "</p>");
        response.getWriter().println("<p>subject:" + context.getSubject() +
        "</p>");
        response.getWriter().println("<p>expires in:" + context.
        getExpiresIn() + "</p>");
        response.getWriter().println("<p>refresh token:" + context.
        getRefreshToken() + "</p>");
        response.getWriter().println("<p>claims json:" + context.
        getClaimsJson() + "</p>");
    }
}
```

The CallbackServlet is used to redirect after login succeeded. It redirects to the
/protected servlet:

```
@WebServlet("/callback")
public class CallbackServlet extends HttpServlet {
private static final Logger LOGGER = Logger.getLogger(CallbackServlet.
class.getName())
@Override
protected void doGet(HttpServletRequest request, HttpServletResponse
response)
throws ServletException, IOException {
LOGGER.log(Level.FINEST, "Enter callback servlet");
```

```
String referrer = (String) request.getSession().getAttribute("Referrer");
String redirectTo = referrer != null ? referrer : request.getContextPath()
+ "/protected";
LOGGER.log(Level.FINEST, "In /callback, redirect to: {0}", redirectTo);
response.sendRedirect(redirectTo);
}
}
```

The UserNameServlet displays the current user info from the SecurityContext:

```
@WebServlet("/username")
@ServletSecurity(@HttpConstraint(rolesAllowed = {"foo", "bar"}))
public class UserNameServlet extends HttpServlet {
private static final Logger LOGGER = Logger.getLogger(UserNameServlet.
class.getName());
@Inject
SecurityContext securityContext;
@Override
protected void doGet(HttpServletRequest request, HttpServletResponse
response) throws ServletException, IOException {
String nameInRequest = request.getUserPrincipal() != null ? request.
getUserPrincipal().getName() : "";
var principal = securityContext.getCallerPrincipal();
LOGGER.log(Level.INFO, "Principal: {0}", principal);
var name = principal.getName();
response.setContentType("text/html");
response.getWriter().println("<h1>UserName Servlet</h1>");
response.getWriter().println("<p>principal name in request userPrincipal:"
+ nameInRequest + "</p>");
response.getWriter().println("<p>principal name:" + name + "</p>");
response.getWriter().println("<p>isCallerInRole('foo'):" + securityContext.
isCallerInRole("foo") + "</p>");
response.getWriter().println("<p>isCallerInRole('bar'):" + securityContext.
isCallerInRole("bar") + "</p>");
}
}
```

To map authenticated users to valid groups, we create a simple `IdentityStore` implementation:

```
@ApplicationScoped
public class AuthorizationIdentityStore implements IdentityStore {
    private static final Logger LOGGER = Logger.getLogger(Authorization
    IdentityStore.class.getName());

    private String email;

    private Map<String, Set<String>> authorization;

    @PostConstruct
    void init() {
        LOGGER.config("IdentityStore.init()");
        try {
            var properties = new Properties();
            properties.load(getClass().getResourceAsStream("/oidc.
            properties"));
            email = properties.getProperty("email", "");
            LOGGER.log(
                    Level.INFO,
                    "email: {0}",
                    new Object[] { email });
        } catch (IOException e) {
            LOGGER.log(Level.SEVERE, "Failed to load oidc.properties", e);
            email = "";
        }
        authorization = Map.of(
            "user", Set.of("foo", "bar"),
            email,  Set.of("foo", "bar")); // user in Google.
    }

    @Inject
    private OpenIdContext context;

    @Override
```

```java
    public Set<ValidationType> validationTypes() {
        return EnumSet.of(PROVIDE_GROUPS);
    }

    @Override
    public Set<String> getCallerGroups(CredentialValidationResult
    validationResult) {
        var principal = validationResult.getCallerPrincipal().getName();
        LOGGER.log(Level.INFO, "Get principal name in validation result:
        {0}", principal);
        LOGGER.log(Level.INFO, "claims json:" + context.getClaimsJson());
        LOGGER.log(Level.INFO, "provider json:" + context.
        getProviderMetadata());
        var issuer = context.getProviderMetadata().getString("issuer");
        if (issuer.endsWith("google.com")) { // As Google returns a long
        numeric user id, we try to use the email address instead
                var email = context.getClaimsJson().getString("email");
                return authorization.get(email) == null ?
                Collections.<String>emptySet() : authorization.get(email);
        } else {
                return authorization.get(principal) == null ?
                Collections.<String>emptySet() : authorization.
                get(principal);
        }
    }
}
```

As Google will return a rather long numeric Google ID, we retrieve the "email" claim from the claims JSON, provided via Jakarta JSON Processing, and compare the Gmail address instead of a long, cryptic surrogate key. For all other providers, for example, Keycloak, we'll use the name of the CallerPrincipal.

To get Google Client ID and Client Secret credentials, you need to create a new application with Google:

1. Go to `https://console.developers.google.com`.

2. Create a new project, for example, "ApressBookDemoApp".

3. Create OAuth 2.0 credentials for the project since Google does not do that automatically. From the sidebar, click the Credentials tab, then click **Create credentials**, and choose **OAuth client ID** from the drop-down.

4. Google will prompt for some information about your application such as the product name, home page, and logo. Most of them are optional. On the next page, select the **Web Application** type, and enter the redirect URL where the Jakarta EE application we will build next will wait for the callback. Enter `http://localhost:8080/callback` as the redirect URL.

5. You then see the Client ID and Client Secret on a screen. Download them as JSON and store it in a secure location.

Edit/create `src/main/resources/oidc.properties` in your Jakarta EE application:

```
issuerUri=https://accounts.google.com
email=<your-email-address>
clientId=<your-cliend-id>
clientSecret=<your-client-secret>
```

Replace the values of `clientId` and `clientSecret` with those in the JSON file from Google and `email` with the email address of a valid test user, for example, your own Gmail address.

Build/run the application with `mvn wildfly:run`.Now you're ready to test it. Visit `http://localhost:8080/public` in the browser.

You see the page:

```
Public Unsecured Servlet
```

Next browse to `http://localhost:8080/protected`.

The first visit will forward you to a Google ID login page. After successfully confirming your Google ID, it'll redirect back to the protected page and show something like

```
Protected Servlet
access token:ya29.a0AfB_...
token type:Bearer
subject:1234567890987654321
expires in:Optional[1234]
refresh token:Optional.empty
claims json:{"sub":"1234567890987654321","name":"John Doel","given_
name":"John","family_name":"Doe","picture":"https://lh3.googleusercontent.
com/a/ABcdefghijklmnopqrstuvwxY-z","email":"john.doel@gmail.com","email_
verified":true,"locale":"xy"}
```

You can also visit `http://localhost:8080/username`.

It will show you something like

```
UserName Servlet
principal name in request userPrincipal:1234567890987654321
principal name:1234567890987654321
isCallerInRole('foo'):true
isCallerInRole('bar'):true
```

The name of the `Principal` is rather cryptic with Google; it's essentially a long number that represents your Google ID.

Open Liberty

Open Liberty is an open source implementation of Eclipse MicroProfile and Jakarta EE from IBM. It is the foundation of the WebSphere Liberty application server.

Open Liberty 22 and above implement the Jakarta EE 10 security specifications.

Social Media Login

The Open Liberty Social Media Login feature provides a form of Single Sign-On (SSO) enabling users to sign into a secured website by using their existing social media accounts.

For example, you can configure the Social Login feature so that users can log into your website with their Facebook or Twitter accounts instead of having to create accounts for your website only. You can enable the Social Login feature for any social media platform that uses the OAuth 2.0 or OpenID Connect 1.0 standard for authorization.

To enable its Social Media 1.0 feature, add the following element to your `server.xml` file, inside the `featureManager` element:

```
<feature> socialLogin-1.0</feature>
```

The Social Media Login feature provides a set of built-in configuration elements for popular social media providers, in addition to generic configuration elements. The following examples show how to configure different scenarios in the `server.xml` file.

Log In with Social Media ID

If multiple social media providers are configured, a customizable selection form is presented. The user can then sign in with a social media provider of their choice. The following example shows how to configure your application to request that the user logs in with their Google ID. You can generate your Google credentials on `https://console.developers.google.com`.

In this example, `your_app_id` and `your_app_secret` are the Google `Client ID` and `Client Secret` credentials for the `formlogin` application.

```
<googleLogin clientId="your_app_id" clientSecret="your_app_secret"  />


<!-- protected applications need to have a security constraint defined -->
<application type="war" id="formlogin" name="formlogin" location="server1/
apps/formlogin.war">
    <application-bnd>
        <security-role name="Employee">
            <special-subject type="ALL_AUTHENTICATED_USERS" />
        </security-role>
    </application-bnd>
</application>
```

Multiple Social Media Providers

You can configure multiple social media providers for users to choose from. The user receives a customizable selection form before authentication with the available providers included on the form. The following example includes a choice of Google, GitHub, Facebook, LinkedIn, and Twitter:

```
<googleLogin clientId="your_app_id" clientSecret="your_app_secret"  />
<githubLogin   clientId="your_app_id"          clientSecret="your_app_
                                               secret"  />

<facebookLogin clientId="your_app_id"          clientSecret="your_app_
                                               secret"  />

<linkedinLogin clientId="your_app_id"          clientSecret="your_app_
                                               secret"  />

<twitterLogin  consumerKey="your_app_id"       consumerSecret="your_app_
                                               secret"/>

<!-- protected applications need to have a security constraint defined -->
<application type="war" id="formlogin" name="formlogin" location="server1/
apps/formlogin.war">
    <application-bnd>
        <security-role name="Employee">
            <special-subject type="ALL_AUTHENTICATED_USERS" />
        </security-role>
    </application-bnd>
</application>
```

Require Users to Be Corporate Registry

You can restrict the presentation of a social media provider to only users who are also in another configured registry. For example, use the `mapToUserRegistry` attribute to configure your application. The user must authenticate through Google and also verify as an existing user in the company LDAP registry:

```
<googleLogin  mapToUserRegistry="true" clientId="your app
id"  clientSecret="your app secret"   />

 <ldapRegistry ...> ... </ldapRegistry>
```

Choose Between Social Media ID and Corporate Registry

You can give users the option of logging in with either a social media provider or with their account on the configured registry. For example, use the enableLocalAuthentication attribute to configure your application so that users can log in with a Google ID or with their account on their company's LDAP registry:

```
<!-- The user is given a choice menu of either Google or LDAP -->
<googleLogin  clientId="your app id"  clientSecret="your app secret" />

<socialLoginWebapp enableLocalAuthentication="true">

<ldapRegistry id="ldap" ...> ... </ldapRegistry>
```

Log In for Only a Subset of Paths or Browsers

To protect only a subset of applications, URLs, or IP addresses, use an authentication filter. The security configuration takes effect only when the conditions in the filter are met. For example, you might want a web application to be secured with the Social Media Login feature and a microservice application secured with the MicroProfile JWT feature, remember from the previous chapter.

In the following example, only requests that contain the /mywebapp URL pattern are secured with Google credentials:

```
<googleLogin  authFilterRef="authFilter1" clientId="your app
id"  clientSecret="your app secret" />

<authFilter id="authFilter1">
    <requestUrl
        id="myUrlFilter"
        urlPattern="/mywebapp"
        matchType="contains" />
</authFilter>
```

Other Social Media Logins

To authenticate with a social media provider that isn't preconfigured with Open Liberty, use the oauth2Login element for OAuth providers or the oidcLogin element for OpenID Connect providers.

These elements supply the configuration details that are needed to work with the provider. The details can usually be obtained from the developer instructions of the social media provider. The following example configures Instagram as the social media provider:

```
<oauth2Login id="instagramLogin" clientId="client_id"
clientSecret="client_secret"
    scope="basic public_content"    responseType="code"
    tokenEndpointAuthMethod="client_secret_post"
    authorizationEndpoint="https://api.instagram.com/oauth/authorize"
    tokenEndpoint="https://api.instagram.com/oauth/access_token"
    userApi="https://api.instagram.com/v1/users/self"
    userNameAttribute="username"
    website="https://www.instagram.com/developer/authentication/">
</oauth2Login>
```

Private Key JWT for Client Authentication

OpenID Connect clients that are configured by using the oidcLogin element in the Social Media Login feature support the private_key_jwt client authentication method with OpenID Connect token endpoints. The process for enabling this in the Social Media Login feature is identical to the OpenID Connect Client 1.0 feature:

```
<oidcLogin id="myOidcClientUsingPrivateKeyJwt"
    tokenEndpointAuthMethod="private_key_jwt"
    tokenEndpointAuthSigningAlgorithm="E512"
    keyAliasName="privatekeyaliasES512"
    ...
/>
```

Use OpenShift Service Accounts to Authenticate and Authorize

The Social Media Login feature can be configured to use OpenShift service accounts to authenticate and authorize protected resource requests. With this configuration, server administrators can secure endpoints, for example, monitoring and metrics endpoints, that might produce sensitive information. The service accounts can authenticate themselves by providing a service account token that was created within the OpenShift cluster in the request. The following example shows how to configure the Social Media Login feature to use OpenShift service accounts as a Single Sign-On provider:

```
<okdServiceLogin />
```

The okdServiceLogin element authenticates all protected resource requests received by Open Liberty. The OpenShift project that the service account is in, is used as the group for the service account for authorization decisions.

Use Active Directory As Authentication Provider

You can configure an Open Liberty server to use Active Directory as an authentication provider for protected resources. The oidcLogin element configures a social login by using the OpenID Connect protocol. With OpenID Connect, the discovery endpoint URL provides the information that the client needs to interact with the authentication provider, which in this case is Active Directory. In the following example, the discoveryEndpoint attribute specifies the endpoint URL for Active Directory:

```
<oidcLogin
    id="liberty-aad-oidc-javaeecafe" clientId="1m2a72a8-Yh32-T56W-95Pq-
    aFNu78491272"
    clientSecret="RaWhKDUcDpngeKCuG14yM6extsMcPXqdUCjYN="
    discoveryEndpoint="https://login.microsoftonline.com/organizations/
    v2.0/.well-known/openid-configuration"
    signatureAlgorithm="RS256"
    userNameAttribute="preferred_username" />
```

Keycloak

Keycloak [66] is an open source identity, access management, and Single Sign-On solution for applications and services. Users can authenticate against Keycloak rather than each individual application, relieving the application from dealing with login forms, authentication, or storing user's identities. Keycloak also offers social logins, support for desktop or mobile apps, and integration into other solutions including LDAP, Active Directory, OAuth, OpenID Connect, or SAML.

History

Keycloak was created by Bill Burke and Stian Thorgersen in 2014. The first release was published in September 2014 after development had started about a year before. In 2016, Red Hat switched the Red Hat SSO product from being based on the PicketLink framework to the Keycloak upstream project, after it had already merged the PicketLink code base into Keycloak.

Since then, Keycloak saw almost manic release cycles and version number changes. At the end of June 2016 around the time Red Hat made Keycloak the basis for its SSO product, version 2.0.0 was released. About a year later, version 3.0.0 came out, followed by Keycloak 4.0.0 in June 2018.

There probably was a bit of an influence by the Java and OpenJDK release cadence pushing out a new major version of the JDK every six months and a Long-Term Service version every two years as of 2021, but not only Keycloak but also other projects by Red Hat like WildFly seemed version-crazy after 2019 because Keycloak 5.0.0 was released in March 2019 with 6.0.0 only a month later. And in November 2019, the version number had jumped to 8. As of August 2021, the most recent Keycloak version is 15.0.2. While the pace at least on the first digit sometimes looks like it slowed down a bit, versions 13–15 were all released in 2021 alone, which makes it look like Red Hat follows a major release nearly every three to four months at the very least, sometimes faster with only minor slowdown in the second half of 2021. The release notes are sometimes just one-liners, which make one wonder how the giant leap of version numbers was justified, but it looks like marketing drives it and the underlying WildFly numbers also increase even more than Keycloak at 25, with WildFly 22–25 all realized in 2021 as well. Starting with version 17.0.0, the default Keycloak distribution switched from WildFly to Quarkus.

On April 10, 2023, Keycloak was accepted by CNCF as an incubating project.

Overview

Keycloak's goal is to make security simple and easy for application developers to secure their enterprise apps and services.

Concepts

Keycloak is based on the following concepts:

- Authentication

- Authorization

- Credentials

- Realm

Authentication

This is a provider example checking, if the request meets the authenticator's requirements:

```
package org.keycloak.authentication;

public interface Authenticator extends Provider {

    /**
     * Initial call for the authenticator.  This method should check the
       current HTTP request to determine if the request
     * satisfies the Authenticator's requirements.  If it doesn't, it
       should send back a challenge response by calling
     * the AuthenticationFlowContext.challenge(Response).  If this
       challenge is a authentication, the action URL
     * of the form must point to
     *
     * /realms/{realm}/login-actions/authenticate?code={session-
       code}&execution={executionId}
     *
     * or
     *
     * /realms/{realm}/login-actions/registration?code={session-
       code}&execution={executionId}
     *
     * {session-code} pertains to the code generated from
       AuthenticationFlowContext.generateAccessCode().  The {executionId}
```

```
 * pertains to the AuthenticationExecutionModel.getId() value obtained
   from AuthenticationFlowContext.getExecution().
 *
 * The action URL will invoke the action() method described below.
 *
 * @param context
 */
void authenticate(AuthenticationFlowContext context);

/**
 * Called from a form action invocation.
 *
 * @param context
 */
void action(AuthenticationFlowContext context);

/**
 * Does this authenticator require that the user has already been
   identified?  That AuthenticatorContext.getUser() is not null?
 *
 * @return
 */
boolean requiresUser();

/**
 * Is this authenticator configured for this user?
 *
 * @param session
 * @param realm
 * @param user
 * @return
 */
boolean configuredFor(KeycloakSession session, RealmModel realm,
UserModel user);

/**
 * Set actions to configure authenticator
```

```
 *
 */
void setRequiredActions(KeycloakSession session, RealmModel realm,
UserModel user);

/**
 * Overwrite this if the authenticator is associated with
 * @return
 */
default List<RequiredActionFactory> getRequiredActions(KeycloakSession
session) {
    return Collections.emptyList();
}

/**
 * Checks if all required actions are configured in the realm and
   are enabled
 * @return
 */
default boolean areRequiredActionsEnabled(KeycloakSession session,
RealmModel realm) {
    for (RequiredActionFactory raf : getRequiredActions(session)) {
        RequiredActionProviderModel rafpm = realm.getRequiredActionProv
        iderByAlias(raf.getId());
        if (rafpm == null) {
            return false;
        }
        if (!rafpm.isEnabled()) {
            return false;
        }
    }
    return true;
}
}
```

Password Policies

Many organizations have special password policies. Keycloak has a rich set of password policies to choose via the Admin Console. There are several password policy types. Hashing the password uses the hash algorithm. The password should match combinations of digits, upper- and lowercase characters, special characters, or a regular expression. As well as common security measures like no to contain the username, not use the same password multiple times or the expiry date, after which the password must be changed.

Authentication Flow

The sequence of actions by a user or service to authenticate in Keycloak is called authentication flow:

```
package org.keycloak.authentication;

public interface AuthenticationFlow {
    String BASIC_FLOW = "basic-flow";
    String FORM_FLOW = "form-flow";
    String CLIENT_FLOW = "client-flow";

    Response processAction(String actionExecution);
    Response processFlow();
    boolean isSuccessful();
    default List<AuthenticationFlowException> getFlowExceptions(){
        return Collections.emptyList();
    }
}
```

Keycloak includes various authentication flows out of the box. Those can be configured as required, and where your application may need something different, you can always create your own authentication flow from scratch or start by copying an existing one.

Figure 5-1 shows the available authentication flows in a browser:

- Cookie

- Identity Provider Redirector

- Forms

    - Username/Password

    - OTP

- Kerberos

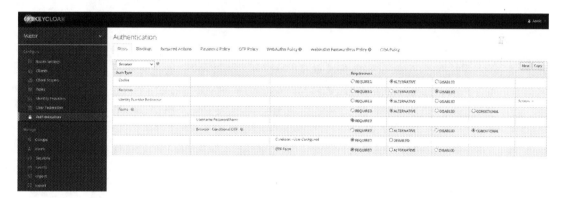

Figure 5-1. *Browser Authentication Flows*

At least one of them has to be enabled for successful authentication.
For Single Sign-On, Keycloak supports two major protocols:

- OpenID Connect (OIDC)

- SAML

OIDC is the preferred method and more commonly used with RESTful APIs, while SAML (which we are going to learn more about in the next section on Shibboleth) gained more popularity with SOAP Web Services, especially in the academic world.

SAML relies on XML messages and documents, while OIDC with REST being format agnostic most often uses JWT for identity and access tokens.

For OIDC, Keycloak defines four main authentication flows:

- Authorization Code Flow – For browser-based or server-side applications.

- Implicit Flow – For browser-based applications, this flow is not as secure as Authorization Code Flow and deprecated as of OAuth 2.1 so it can be used for backward compatibility, but it's not recommended anymore.

- Client Credentials Grant – For consumers of RESTful web services, involves storing a secret, so the clients should trust the services they consume.

Authorization

Keycloak supports multiple authorization policies and allows to combine different access control mechanisms like

- Attribute-based access control (ABAC)

- Role-based access control (RBAC)

- User-based access control (UBAC)

- Context-based access control (CBAC)

- Rule-based access control

- Time-based access control

- Custom access control mechanisms via a Policy Provider SPI

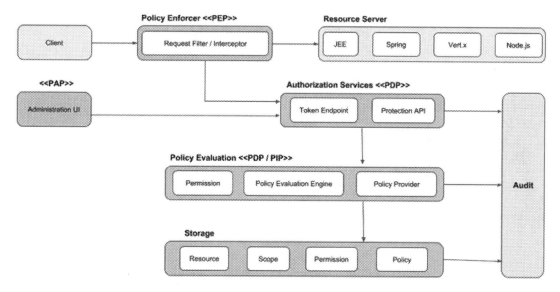

Figure 5-2. *Keycloak Authorization Architecture*

Credentials

Credentials are pieces of data that Keycloak uses to verify the identity of a user. Some examples are passwords, one-time passwords, digital certificates, iris scans, or fingerprints.

Realm

A realm allows to manage a set of users, credentials, roles, and groups. A user belongs to and logs into a realm. Realms are isolated from one another and can only manage and authenticate users they control.

Features

The main features of Keycloak are as follows:

- Clients (per application)
- Events
- Identity Providers

- OpenID Connect

- SAML

- Social Login – Enable login with Google, GitHub, Facebook, Twitter, and other social networks

- Security Defenses

- UI (Themes)

- User Management

  - Users

  - Groups

  - Roles

- User Federation

  - LDAP

  - Active Directory

  - Custom Providers

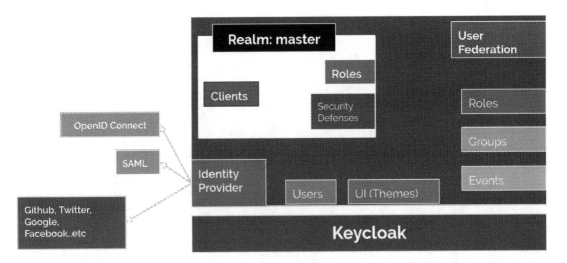

Figure 5-3. *Keycloak Features*

Clients

Clients in Keycloak are entities (applications or services) that wish to authenticate a user within a realm. They can also request identity information or an access token so that they can securely invoke other services across the network secured by Keycloak. During the authentication process, the client needs to send its ID and secret. These credentials are obtained by registering the client in the authentication server.

With many applications to secure and maintain in an organization, it can become tedious to configure protocol mappers and scope for all these clients. Keycloak lets you define shared client configurations in a client template.

Events

Keycloak provides extensive auditing functionalities. Every interaction can be recorded and reviewed. There are two kinds of events:

- Login events

- Admin events

Login events occur every time a user-related action around authentication takes place, for example, login, logout, login attempts that were unsuccessful, or when a user account gets updated. Admin events are triggered by every change via the Admin API, either via Admin Console, REST API, or Command-Line Interface. A Listener SPI allows you to create plug-ins and listen for these events.

Here is an example EventListenerProvider implementation writing events to System.out:

```
public class SysoutEventListenerProvider implements EventListenerProvider {

    private Set<EventType> excludedEvents;
    private Set<OperationType> excludedAdminOperations;

    public SysoutEventListenerProvider(Set<EventType> excludedEvents,
    Set<OperationType> excludedAdminOpearations) {
        this.excludedEvents = excludedEvents;
        this.excludedAdminOperations = excludedAdminOpearations;
    }
```

```java
@Override
public void onEvent(Event event) {
    // Ignore excluded events
    if (excludedEvents != null && excludedEvents.contains(event.
    getType())) {
        return;
    } else {
        System.out.println("EVENT: " + toString(event));
    }
}

@Override
public void onEvent(AdminEvent event, boolean includeRepresentation) {
    // Ignore excluded operations
    if (excludedAdminOperations != null && excludedAdminOperations.
    contains(event.getOperationType())) {
        return;
    } else {
        System.out.println("EVENT: " + toString(event));
    }
}

private String toString(Event event) {
    StringBuilder sb = new StringBuilder();

    sb.append("type=");
    sb.append(event.getType());
    sb.append(", realmId=");
    sb.append(event.getRealmId());
    sb.append(", clientId=");
    sb.append(event.getClientId());
    sb.append(", userId=");
    sb.append(event.getUserId());
    sb.append(", ipAddress=");
    sb.append(event.getIpAddress());

    if (event.getError() != null) {
        sb.append(", error=");
```

```
        sb.append(event.getError());
    }

    if (event.getDetails() != null) {
        for (Map.Entry<String, String> e : event.getDetails().
        entrySet()) {
            sb.append(", ");
            sb.append(e.getKey());
            if (e.getValue() == null || e.getValue().indexOf(' ') ==
            -1) {
                sb.append("=");
                sb.append(e.getValue());
            } else {
                sb.append("='");
                sb.append(e.getValue());
                sb.append("'");
            }
        }
    }

    return sb.toString();
}

private String toString(AdminEvent adminEvent) {
    StringBuilder sb = new StringBuilder();

    sb.append("operationType=");
    sb.append(adminEvent.getOperationType());
    sb.append(", realmId=");
    sb.append(adminEvent.getAuthDetails().getRealmId());
    sb.append(", clientId=");
    sb.append(adminEvent.getAuthDetails().getClientId());
    sb.append(", userId=");
    sb.append(adminEvent.getAuthDetails().getUserId());
    sb.append(", ipAddress=");
    sb.append(adminEvent.getAuthDetails().getIpAddress());
    sb.append(", resourcePath=");
    sb.append(adminEvent.getResourcePath());
```

```java
        if (adminEvent.getError() != null) {
            sb.append(", error=");
            sb.append(adminEvent.getError());
        }

        return sb.toString();
    }

    @Override
    public void close() {
    }

}
```

And its factory:

```java
public class SysoutEventListenerProviderFactory implements
EventListenerProviderFactory {

    private Set<EventType> excludedEvents;
    private Set<OperationType> excludedAdminOperations;

    @Override
    public EventListenerProvider create(KeycloakSession session) {
        return new SysoutEventListenerProvider(excludedEvents,
        excludedAdminOperations);
    }

    @Override
    public void init(Config.Scope config) {
        String[] excludes = config.getArray("exclude-events");
        if (excludes != null) {
            excludedEvents = new HashSet<>();
            for (String e : excludes) {
                excludedEvents.add(EventType.valueOf(e));
            }
        }

        String[] excludesOperations = config.getArray("excludesOpe
        rations");
```

```
    if (excludesOperations != null) {
        excludedAdminOperations = new HashSet<>();
        for (String e : excludesOperations) {
            excludedAdminOperations.add(OperationType.valueOf(e));
        }
    }
}

@Override
public void postInit(KeycloakSessionFactory factory) {

}
@Override
public void close() {
}

@Override
public String getId() {
    return "sysout";
}
}
```

User Federation

When your organization has a user database, Keycloak allows us to synchronize with it. By default, it supports LDAP and Active Directory, but you can create custom extensions for any identity store using the Keycloak User storage API.

Keycloak can also act as a proxy between your users and external identity providers.

Social Identity Providers

A social identity provider can delegate authentication to a trusted social media account. Keycloak includes support for social networks like Google, Facebook, Twitter, GitHub, LinkedIn, Microsoft, and Stack Overflow.

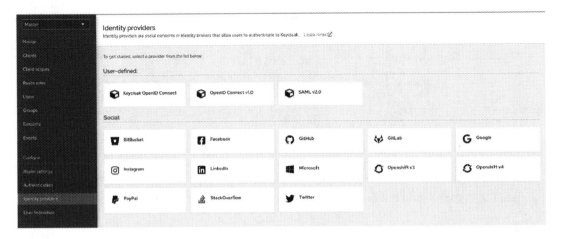

Figure 5-4. *Social Identity Providers*

Facebook

1. Click ***Identity Providers*** in the menu.

2. From the *Add provider* list, select Facebook. Keycloak displays the configuration page for the Facebook identity provider.

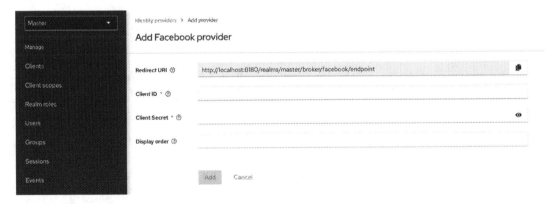

Figure 5-5. *Add Facebook As Identity Provider*

3. Copy the value of Redirect URI to your clipboard.

4. In a separate browser tab, follow the Facebook Developer Guide's instructions to create a project and client in Facebook.

   a) Ensure your app is of type website-type.

   b) Enter the `Redirect URI`'s value into the Site URL of the Facebook Website settings block.

   c) Ensure the app is public.

5. Enter the `Client ID` and `Client Secret` values from your Facebook app into the `Client ID` and `Client Secret` fields in Keycloak.

6. Click *Add*.

7. Enter the required scopes into the *Default Scopes* field. By default, Keycloak uses the `email` scope. See Graph API for more information about Facebook scopes.

By default, Keycloak sends profile requests to `graph.facebook.com/me?fields=id,name,email,first_name,last_name`.

The response only contains the `id`, `name`, `email`, `first_name`, and `last_name` fields. To fetch additional fields from the Facebook profile, add a corresponding scope and add the field name in the Additional user's profile fields configuration option.

Spring Security

Spring Security [67] is a security framework that works especially well with the Spring Framework or Spring Web MVC and more recently Reactive applications using Spring Flux as well. Spring Security is a continuation of Acegi Security, a powerful security framework. But the problem was it required a lot of cumbersome XML configuration to realize it. Spring embraced it into the family from version 2.0 and, since then, refined it to its present state. Although the XML configuration is still possible, Spring's new spirit of convention over configuration also influenced it the same way we also see in Jakarta EE. It is possible to perform all security configurations with annotation rather than XML, although the provision is still there for backward compatibility and to leverage certain flexibility. Its primary goal is to handle authentication and authorization for web requests and method invocations.

History

Spring Security began two decades ago, in late 2003, as "The Acegi Security System for Spring," initially created by Ben Alex, based on questions asked on the Spring Developers' mailing list whether there had been any Spring-based security implementation. Back then, the Spring community was relatively small, and Spring itself had only existed as a SourceForge project from early 2003. The answer to the question was that it was worthwhile, although a lack of time and resources prevented its exploration back then.

With that in mind, a simple security implementation was built but remained unreleased. A few weeks later, another member of the Spring community asked about security, and this code was offered to them.

Other similar questions followed, and by January 2004, around 20 people were using the code. These initial users were joined by others who suggested a SourceForge project of its own, which was created in March 2004.

Back then, the project didn't have its own authentication modules. J2EE Container Managed Security was used for the authentication process, with the first version of Acegi Security instead focusing on authorization. This was suitable at first, but as more users requested support for additional containers, the limitation of container-specific authentication realm interfaces became evident. Adding new JARs to the container's Classpath also caused issues, which was a common source of admin confusion and misconfiguration. Acegi Security authentication services were introduced. And around a year later, Acegi Security became an official Spring Framework subproject. The 1.0.0 final release was published in May 2006 – after more than two and a half years of production use by numerous projects and hundreds of improvement requests and community contributions. Acegi Security became an official Spring project toward the end of 2007 and was rebranded to "Spring Security."

Overview

Spring Security is based on three main concepts:

- Authentication

- Authorization

- Servlet Filters

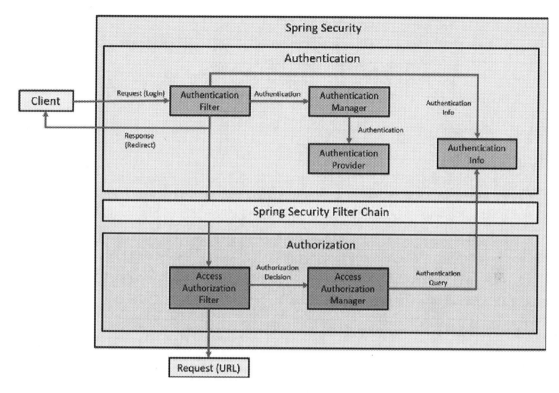

Figure 5-6. *Spring Security Authentication/Authorization Flow*

Authentication

The main interface for authentication in Spring Security is AuthenticationManager, which has just one method, authenticate().

```
public interface AuthenticationManager {
  Authentication authenticate(Authentication authentication)
    throws AuthenticationException;
}
```

The most common implementation of AuthenticationManager is ProviderManager, which delegates to a chain of AuthenticationProvider instances. An AuthenticationProvider is similar to an AuthenticationManager, but it has an extra method allowing a caller to check whether it supports a particular authentication type.

```
public interface AuthenticationProvider {
    Authentication authenticate(Authentication authentication)
                throws AuthenticationException;

    boolean supports(Class<?> authentication);
}
```

Authorization

The main element in Spring Security for authorization is `AccessDecisionManager`. There are three default implementations provided by the framework, and all of them use a chain of `AccessDecisionVoter` instances, a bit like the `ProviderManager` does with instances of `AuthenticationProvider`.

An `AccessDecisionVoter<S>` uses an `Authentication` (a principal) and a secure object, decorated by a `ConfigAttribute`:

```
boolean supports(ConfigAttribute attribute);

boolean supports(Class<?> clazz);

int vote(Authentication authentication, S object,
        Collection<ConfigAttribute> attributes);
```

The interface `ConfigAttribute` encapsulates access information metadata in a secured resource. Figure 5-7 shows the hierarchy of configuration attributes.

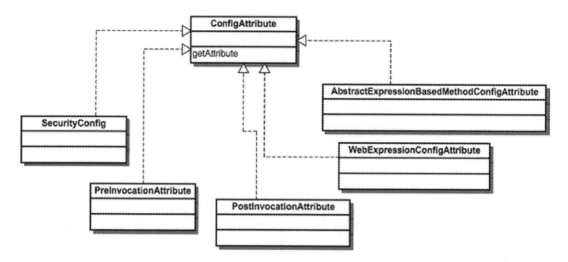

Figure 5-7. *Config Attribute Hierarchy*

Servlet Filters

The web tier of Spring Security is based on standard Jakarta EE Servlet Filters, although as of Spring Security and Framework 5, that is at most Jakarta EE 8. The Spring Security filter chain builds on several filters to cover different security constraints of a web application. Figure 5-8 shows the typical chain of these filters for a single HTTP request.

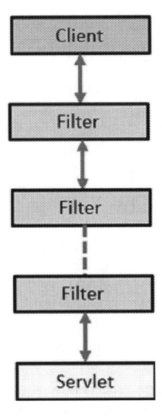

Figure 5-8. *Filter Chain for a Single HTTP Request*

For the container, Spring Security is basically a single filter, composed of multiple filters for different purposes. Spring Security is installed as a single filter in the chain. This filter, named `FilterChainProxy`, contains all the details about the different security filters available through the security filter chain. Using the Proxy Pattern, it determines which `SecurityFilterChain` will be invoked for an incoming request.

Here's an example:

```
<bean id="filterChainProxy" class="org.springframework.security.web.
FilterChainProxy">
  <sec:filter-chain-map path-type="ant">
    <sec:filter-chain pattern="/webServices/**" filters="
        securityContextPersistenceFilterWithASCFalse,
        basicAuthenticationFilter,
        exceptionTranslationFilter,
        filterSecurityInterceptor" />
```

```
    <sec:filter-chain pattern="/**" filters="
        securityContextPersistenceFilterWithASCTrue,
        formLoginFilter,
        exceptionTranslationFilter,
        filterSecurityInterceptor" />
    </sec:filter-chain-map>
</bean>
```

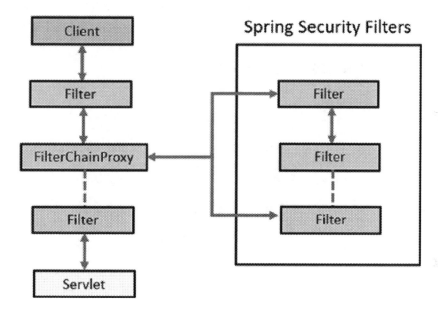

Figure 5-9. *Filter Chain Proxy*

However, FilterChainProxy is not called directly but via the DelegatingFilterProxy filter. Using it, you will see something like this in the web.xml file of your web application:

```
<filter>
    <filter-name>myFilter</filter-name>
    <filter-class>org.springframework.web.filter.DelegatingFilterProxy</filter-class>
</filter>
```

```
<filter-mapping>
    <filter-name>myFilter</filter-name>
    <url-pattern>/*</url-pattern>
</filter-mapping>
```

Social Login

OAuth 2 support for authentication providers like Facebook, Google, and GitHub is built into Spring Security 5. Here are the examples of OAuth 2 client configuration for them.

Configure Authentication Provider

First, configure the social authentication provider of your choice.

Facebook

Configure `Client ID` and `Client Secret` in your `application.properties`:

```
spring.security.oauth2.client.registration.facebook.client-id =
<Facebook app id>
spring.security.oauth2.client.registration.facebook.client-secret =
<Facebook app secret>
```

To get Facebook App ID and App secret credentials, you will need to create a new application with Facebook at `https://developers.facebook.com/apps/`.

Configure HTTP Security

Next use the `@EnableWebSecurity` annotation and configure the `HTTPSecurity` object.

Create a new Java class in your project and make it extend the `WebSecurityConfigurerAdapter`. Annotate this class with a `@EnableWebSecurity` annotation:

```
import org.springframework.security.config.annotation.web.builders.
HttpSecurity;
import org.springframework.security.config.annotation.web.configuration.
EnableWebSecurity;
import org.springframework.security.config.annotation.web.configuration.
WebSecurityConfigurerAdapter;
```

```
@EnableWebSecurity
public class WebSecurity extends WebSecurityConfigurerAdapter {

    @Override
    protected void configure(HttpSecurity http) throws Exception {
        http.authorizeRequests()
                .antMatchers("/").permitAll()
                .anyRequest().authenticated()
                .and()
                .oauth2Login()
                .and()
                .logout().logoutSuccessUrl("/");
    }
}
```

That will make our application redirect users to a social login provider for authentication. Once a user successfully authenticates with the social login provider, they will be redirected back to the protected page of our application they have initially requested. Notice we also enabled the logout functionality and configured the logout successful URL.

Create a Protected Page

The following example will create a Controller class with a single resource called "users":

```
import org.springframework.security.core.annotation.
AuthenticationPrincipal;
import org.springframework.security.oauth2.core.user.OAuth2User;
import org.springframework.stereotype.Controller;
import org.springframework.ui.Model;
import org.springframework.web.bind.annotation.GetMapping;

@Controller
public class UsersController {

    @GetMapping("/users")
    public String getUser(Model model, @AuthenticationPrincipal OAuth2User
    principal) {
```

```
        if (principal != null) {
            model.addAttribute("name", principal.getAttribute("name"));
        }

        return "user";
    }

}
```

When the /users resource is requested, our application will redirect users
to authenticate with a social login provider. If authentication is successful, the
user will be redirected back to the /users resource. Because authentication was
successful, we can get information about the currently authenticated user via the @
AuthenticationPrincipal annotation, which will help us access the OAuth2User object.
The OAuth2User is a principal object we can obtain details for.

Micronaut Security

Micronaut Security is a security framework for Micronaut applications [68]. Micronaut is
generally similar to Spring Boot but has a better startup time in most cases. The JAR files
are smaller, and it consumes less memory at runtime.

Of course each "Microframework" tries to optimize performance with every new
version, and those differences may vary from release to release.

Features

The main features of Micronaut Security include

- Authentication

- Authorization

- Security Rules

- Security Events

- Token Propagation

Secure a Micronaut Application with Google

After you installed Micronaut, follow the step-by-step guide: `https://guides.micronaut.io/latest/micronaut-oauth2-oidc-google-gradle-java.html`

If you prefer Maven, under step 4, call

```
mn create-app example.micronaut.micronautguide --build=maven --lang=java
```

Apache Shiro

Apache Shiro is an open source security framework that provides application developers intuitive, simple ways of supporting

- Authentication

- Authorization

- Cryptography

- Session Management

The word "shiro" means castle in Japanese.

History

Shiro was created out of developer's needs not met by standards around that time. Les Hazlewood and Jeremy Haile created a security framework named JSecurity at SourceForge between 2004 and 2008 because they could not find an existing Java security framework suitable for their needs and JAAS (we already learned about in Chapter 1) did not work well for them. Their effort started roughly around the same time as Acegi Security in 2004, also at SourceForge, which was then the largest independent open source hosting community, a lot like GitHub is now. JSecurity attracted more committers including Peter Ledbrook, Alan Ditzel, or Tim Veil.

In 2008, JSecurity was submitted to the Apache Software Foundation and accepted into its Incubator program mentored toward becoming a top-level Apache project. Under the ASF Incubator, JSecurity was first renamed Ki (pronounced "Key"), only to be soon renamed Shiro due to trademark concerns. The project grew in the Apache

Incubator, adding Kalle Korhonen as committer. In July 2010, the Shiro team released its official version 1.0. Following the release of the first version, the Shiro project created a Project Management Committee (PMC) and elected Les Hazlewood as its chair. On September 22, 2010, Shiro became a top-level Apache project.

Overview

Shiro is based on three core concepts:

- Subject
- SecurityManager
- Realm

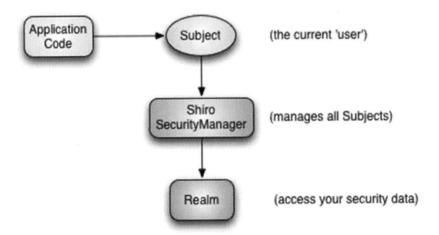

Figure 5-10. *Shiro Concepts*

Subject

The Subject is basically a "view" of the current user. While "User" suggests a human person, a "Subject" can also be a service or a corporate entity.

SecurityManager

The SecurityManager, not to be mistaken for the API type soon to be removed from the JDK, is the central element of Shiro's architecture.

Realm

A realm manages a set of users, roles, and permissions. A user belongs to and logs into a realm. Realms are isolated from one another and can only manage and authenticate users they control. Realms usually have a direct correlation with a data source, for example, a database, LDAP directory, file system, or a similar resource.

Features

Figure 5-11 shows the main concerns of Shiro as well as other supporting features.

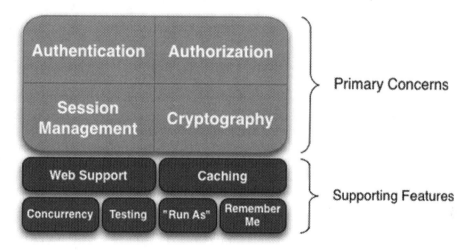

Figure 5-11. *Shiro Features*

- Authentication across multiple pluggable data sources including

  - LDAP/Active Directory

  - JDBC

  - JNDI

- Authorization based on roles or fine-grained permissions

  - Know if a user is assigned a certain role or not.

  - Know if a user is allowed to do something or not.

- Session Management – Use in both web and "serverless," or any environment where Single Sign-On, clustered, or distributed sessions are required.

- Cryptography – Secure data with cryptographic algorithms beyond the standard Java ciphers and hashes, yet easy to use.

Other supporting Shiro features are as follows:

- Web Support – Helps secure web applications

- Caching, to ensure applications run fast and efficient

- Concurrency, supporting multithreaded applications

- Test Support – Helping to write unit or integration tests to check if your applications are as secure as expected

- "Run As", allowing users to assume the identity of another user, a bit like the "sudo" command on Linux

- "Remember Me" to remember users across sessions, allowing them to only log in when required, for example, if the session expired

Authentication

Shiro aims to make authentication intuitive and easy to use despite a variety of features; these are the highlights:

- Subject Based

- Single Method Call

- Detailed Exception Hierarchy

- Built-in "Remember Me"

- Pluggable Data Sources

- Using Multiple Realms

Steps to Authenticate a Subject

Authenticating a Subject can be broken down into three steps:

1. Collect the Subject's submitted principals and credentials.

2. Submit the principals and credentials for authentication.

3. If the submission was successful, grant access; otherwise, retry authentication or block access.

Here's how to use Shiro's API for these steps:

Collect the Subject's submitted principals and credentials

```
//Most common scenario of username/password pair:
UsernamePasswordToken token = new UsernamePasswordToken(username,
password);

//"Remember Me" built-in:
token.setRememberMe(true);
```

In this case, we used the UsernamePasswordToken, supporting the most common username/password authentication approach. This is an implementation of Shiro's org.apache.shiro.authc.AuthenticationToken interface, which is the base interface of Shiro's authentication system to represent submitted principals and credentials.

Shiro does not care how you acquire this information: perhaps the data was entered via HTML form, or maybe retrieved from an HTTP header, or maybe through command-line arguments. The process of an application collecting information from users is completely decoupled from Shiro's AuthenticationToken concept.

You may construct and represent AuthenticationToken instances any way you like; it is protocol agnostic.

This example also shows that we have indicated that we wish Shiro to perform "Remember Me" services for authentication.

Authorization

Authorization has three main elements:

- Permission

- Role

- User (Subject)

Permissions

Permissions are an essential aspect of security policies. They allow what can be done in an application. Common permissions for data elements are Create, Read, Update, and Delete, commonly known as *CRUD*.

Granularity

Shiro allows very fine-grained permissions where required, in any granularity, for example:

- Resource level – The broadest definition, for example, allowing a user to edit customer records or finances

- Instance level – Permissions that are specific to a particular instance of a resource, not just the general type, such as allowing a user to access the customer records of IBM, but not Red Hat

- Attribute level – Allowing to specify permissions for an attribute of an instance or resource, for example, the home address or work address of an IBM employee

Here's a permission example. We check if users have permission to print using a "Colour Printer" and those who do will see a "print" button, the others don't. This is an example of an instance level permission.

```
Subject currentUser = SecurityUtils.getSubject();

Permission printPermission = new PrinterPermission("ColourPrinter"
,"print");

If (currentUser.isPermitted(printPermission)) {
    // show the print button?)
```

```
} else {
    // don't show the button?
}
```

Users

A user or "Subject" (because as mentioned, it can also be a service or corporate entity) can be any actor in your application. In most cases, you'd obtain the current Subject by using org.apache.shiro.SecurityUtils:

```
Subject currentUser = SecurityUtils.getSubject();
```

Roles

Remember the RBAC from Chapter 2; roles are a set of permissions, allowing to assign permissions to a role instead of each individual user.

Shiro provides two types of roles:

- Implicit roles

- Explicit roles

Application role checks are usually the assignment of an **implicit** role. A user with the role "administrator" can view customer data. The names of the roles are not necessarily related to a business requirement or scenario, while an **explicit** role already comes with permissions it needs. For example, a user with the role "editor" has the "publish chapters" permission assigned to it.

```
Realm realm = new MyPublishingRealm();
SecurityManager securityManager = new DefaultSecurityManager(realm);

SecurityUtils.setSecurityManager(securityManager);
Subject currentUser = SecurityUtils.getSubject();

if (!currentUser.isAuthenticated()) {
  UsernamePasswordToken token
    = new UsernamePasswordToken("user", "password");
  token.setRememberMe(true);
  try {
      currentUser.login(token);
```

167

```java
    } catch (UnknownAccountException uae) {
        log.error("Username Not Found!", uae);
    } catch (IncorrectCredentialsException ice) {
        log.error("Invalid Credentials!", ice);
    } catch (LockedAccountException lae) {
        log.error("Your Account is Locked!", lae);
    } catch (AuthenticationException ae) {
        log.error("Unexpected Error!", ae);
    }
}

log.info("User [" + currentUser.getPrincipal() + "] logged in
successfully.");

if (currentUser.hasRole("admin")) {
    log.info("Welcome Admin");
} else if(currentUser.hasRole("editor")) {
    log.info("Welcome, Editor!");
} else if(currentUser.hasRole("author")) {
    log.info("Welcome, Author");
} else {
    log.info("Welcome, Guest");
}

if(currentUser.isPermitted("chapters:write")) {
    log.info("You can write a chapter");
} else {
    log.info("You are not permitted to write a chapter!");
}

if(currentUser.isPermitted("chapters:save")) {
    log.info("You can save chapters");
} else {
    log.info("You can not save chapters");
}

if(currentUser.isPermitted("chapters:publish")) {
```

```
    log.info("You can publish chapters");
} else {
    log.info("You can not publish chapters");
}

Session session = currentUser.getSession();
session.setAttribute("key", "value");
String value = (String) session.getAttribute("key");
if (value.equals("value")) {
    log.info("Retrieved the correct value! [" + value + "]");
}

currentUser.logout();
```

Session Management

Once we got the current user, we can retrieve their session:

```
Session session = currentUser.getSession();
session.setAttribute( "key", "value" );
```

The Session is a Shiro-specific instance containing most of what you'd know from the Jakarta Servlet HttpSession with a few extras, and it is independent of an HTTP environment.

Inside a web application, the Session will be HttpSession based. But in a non-web environment, Shiro will automatically use its own Session Management by default. This means you get to use the same API in your applications, regardless of the deployment environment. This opens new possibilities especially for "serverless" applications, as the application requiring sessions does not need to use HttpSession or EJB Stateful Session Beans.

Cryptography

The main cryptography aspects of Shiro are as follows:

- Simplicity

- Cipher features

- Hash features

Social Login

The following example shows how to handle Facebook login for a Shiro application.

Create a Facebook App

To get Facebook App ID and App secret credentials, you will need to create a new application with Facebook at `https://developers.facebook.com/apps/`.

Example Code

Facebook user details:

```
package com.example.facebook;

/**
* Simple class for holding Facebook user data
*/
class FacebookUserDetails {
// jsonString Expected to be something like this:
// email
// {
// "education": [{
// "school": {
// "id": "123456789012345",
// "name": "Vienna University of Technology "
// },
// "type": "Graduate School",
// "with": [{
// "id": "123456789",
// "name": "BRG"
// }]
// }],
// "first_name": "Werner",
// "id": "123456789",
// "last_name": "Keil",
// "link":
// "http://www.facebook.com/profile.php?id=123456789",
```

```java
// "locale": "de_DE",
// "name": "Werner Keil ",
// "updated_time": "2023-05-15T14:51:05+0000",
// "verified": true
// }
private String jsonString;

public FacebookUserDetails(String fbResponse){
jsonString = fbResponse;
JSONObject respJson;
try {
  respJson = new JSONObject(fbResponse);
  this.id = respJson.getString("id");
  this.firstName = respjson.has("first_name") ? respJson.getString
  ("first_name") : " no name" + id;
  this.lastName = respJson.has("last_name") ? respJson.getString
  ("last_name") : "";
  this.email = respJson.has("email") ? respJson.getString("email") :
  "-no email-";
} catch (JSONException e) {
  System.out.println( "fbResponse:"+fbResponse );
  throw new RuntimeException(e);
}

}


public String toString(){
  return jsonString;
}

public String getId() {
  return id;
}

public void setId(String id) {
  this.id = id;
}
```

```java
public String getFirstName() {
  return firstName;
}

public void setFirstName(String firstName) {
  this.firstName = firstName;
}

public String getLastName() {
  return lastName;
}

public void setLastName(String lastName) {
  this.lastName = lastName;
}

public String getEmail() {
  return email;
}

public void setEmail(String email) {
  this.email = email;
}
}
```

Facebook Realm:

```java
package com.example.facebook;

import java.io.ByteArrayOutputStream;
import java.io.IOException;
import java.io.InputStream;
import java.net.MalformedURLException;
import java.net.URL;
import java.util.HashMap;
import java.util.Map;
import java.util.Properties;

import org.apache.shiro.authc.AuthenticationException;
import org.apache.shiro.authc.AuthenticationInfo;
```

```java
import org.apache.shiro.authc.AuthenticationToken;
import org.apache.shiro.authz.AuthorizationInfo;
import org.apache.shiro.realm.AuthorizingRealm;
import org.apache.shiro.subject.PrincipalCollection;

public class FacebookRealm extends AuthorizingRealm {

private static final Properties props = new FacebookProperties().
getProperties();
private static final String APP_SECRET = props.get("fbAppSecret").
toString();
private static final String APP_ID = props.get("fbAppId").toString();
private static final String REDIRECT_URL = props.get("fbLoginRedirectURL").
toString();

@Override
public boolean supports(AuthenticationToken token) {
if (token instanceof FacebookToken) {
return true;
}
return false;
}

@Override
protected AuthorizationInfo doGetAuthorizationInfo(PrincipalCollection
principals) {
return new FacebookAuthorizationInfo();
}

@Override
protected AuthenticationInfo doGetAuthenticationInfo(AuthenticationToken
token) throws AuthenticationException {
FacebookToken facebookToken = (FacebookToken) token;

if (facebookToken.getCode() != null && facebookToken.getCode().trim().
length() > 0) {
URL authUrl;
try {
```

```
authUrl = new URL("https://graph.facebook.com/oauth/access_token?" +
"client_id=" + APP_ID
+ "&redirect_uri=" + REDIRECT_URL + "&client_secret=" + APP_SECRET +
"&code="
+ facebookToken.getCode());

String authResponse = readURL(authUrl);
System.out.println(authResponse);
String accessToken = getPropsMap(authResponse).get("access_token");
URL url = new URL("https://graph.facebook.com/me?access_token=" +
accessToken);
String fbResponse = readURL(url);
FacebookUserDetails userDetails = new FacebookUserDetails(fbResponse);
return new FacebookAuthenticationInfo(userDetails, this.getName());
} catch (MalformedURLException e1) {
e1.printStackTrace();
throw new AuthenticationException(e1);
} catch (IOException ioe) {
ioe.printStackTrace();
throw new AuthenticationException(ioe);
} catch (Throwable e) {
e.printStackTrace();
}
}
return null;
}

private String readURL(URL url) throws IOException {
ByteArrayOutputStream baos = new ByteArrayOutputStream();
InputStream is = url.openStream();
int r;
while ((r = is.read()) != -1) {
baos.write(r);
}
return new String(baos.toByteArray());
}
```

```
private Map<String, String> getPropsMap(String someString) {
String[] pairs = someString.split("&");
Map<String, String> props = new HashMap<>();
for (String propPair : pairs) {
  String[] pair = propPair.split("=");
  props.put(pair[0], pair[1]);
}
return props;
}
}
```

The CredentialsMatcher class shouldn't have to do much, as Facebook is matching the credentials for us:

```
package com.example.facebook;

import org.apache.shiro.authc.AuthenticationInfo;
import org.apache.shiro.authc.AuthenticationToken;
import org.apache.shiro.authc.credential.CredentialsMatcher;

public class FacebookCredentialsMatcher implements CredentialsMatcher {

/**
* Just confirms the right kind of token, credentials checking is done by
facebook OAuth
*/
@Override
public boolean doCredentialsMatch(AuthenticationToken token,
AuthenticationInfo info) {
if(info instanceof FacebookAuthenticationInfo){
return true;
}
return false;
}

}
```

Then create a Facebook token class, used to hold the "code" provided by Facebook:

```java
package com.example.facebook;

import org.apache.shiro.authc.AuthenticationToken;

public class FacebookToken implements AuthenticationToken {

private static final long serialVersionUID = 1L;
private final String code;

public FacebookToken(String code){
  this.code = code;
}

@Override
public Object getPrincipal() {
  return null; // Unknown - Facebook does the login
}

@Override
public Object getCredentials() {
  return null; // credentials handled by Facebook - we don't need them
}

public String getCode() {
  return code;
}

public void setCode(String code) {
  this.code = code;
}
}
```

A FacebookAuthenticationInfo class:

```java
package com.example.facebook;

import java.util.ArrayList;
import java.util.Collection;
```

```
import org.apache.shiro.authc.AuthenticationInfo;
import org.apache.shiro.subject.PrincipalCollection;
import org.apache.shiro.subject.SimplePrincipalCollection;

public class FacebookAuthenticationInfo implements AuthenticationInfo {

private static final long serialVersionUID = 1L;

private PrincipalCollection principalCollection;

public FacebookAuthenticationInfo(FacebookUserDetails facebookUserDetails,
String realmName){
Collection<String> principals = new ArrayList<>();
principals.add(facebookUserDetails.getId());
principals.add(facebookUserDetails.getFirstName()+" "+facebookUserDetails.
getLastName());
this.principalCollection = new SimplePrincipalCollection(principals,
realmName);
}

@Override
public PrincipalCollection getPrincipals() {
  return principalCollection;
}

@Override
public Object getCredentials() {
  return null; // no credentials required
}
}
```

Now create a Facebook login servlet to handle the redirection from Facebook:

```
package com.example.facebook;

import java.io.IOException;

import javax.servlet.ServletException;
import javax.servlet.http.HttpServlet;
```

```java
import javax.servlet.http.HttpServletRequest;
import javax.servlet.http.HttpServletResponse;

import org.apache.shiro.SecurityUtils;
import org.apache.shiro.authc.AuthenticationException;

import uk.co.mrdw.shiro.facebook.FacebookToken;

/**
 * Simple Facebook Login Handler, using Apache Shiro
 */
public class FacebookLoginServlet extends HttpServlet {

private static final long serialVersionUID = 1L;

protected void doGet(HttpServletRequest request, HttpServletResponse
response) throws ServletException, IOException {
  String code = request.getParameter("code");
  FacebookToken facebookToken = new FacebookToken(code);
 try {
SecurityUtils.getSubject().login(facebookToken);
response.sendRedirect(response.encodeRedirectURL("index.jsp"));
}
catch(AuthenticationException ae){
  throw new ServletException(ae);
}
}

protected void doPost(HttpServletRequest request, HttpServletResponse
response) throws ServletException,
IOException {
  System.out.println("Error during doPost ...");
}
}
```

shiro.ini:

```
[main]
 realmA = com.example.dao.RoleSecurityJdbcRealm
 fbCredentialsMatcher = com.example.shiro.facebook.
FacebookCredentialsMatcher
 realmB = com.example.shiro.facebook.FacebookRealm
 realmB.credentialsMatcher = $fbCredentialsMatcher
 securityManager.realms = $realmA, $realmB.ini:
```

Scribe

The Scribe project has built-in support for many popular services that use OAuth, such as Facebook, Twitter, Google, or LinkedIn. It has very few external dependencies, mainly Apache Commons Codec, allowing seamless integration into solutions without risk of dependency clash many larger and more complex solutions bear.

Calling an OAuth provider in Scribe can be as easy as the following one-liner shows:

```
OAuthService service = new ServiceBuilder()
                            .provider(LinkedInApi.class)
                            .apiKey(YOUR_API_KEY)
                            .apiSecret(YOUR_API_SECRET)
                            .build();
```

Until version 0.6 of Agorava, Scribe was at the heart of its OAuth functionality. From Agorava 0.7 onward, it was replaced by JBoss PicketLink.

While the latter is no longer actively developed by Red Hat and was superseded by Keycloak, Scribe is still maintained and gets updates approximately once a year, the last one in January 2023.

Legacy Frameworks

Some of these frameworks are still in use by products and services, but they are no longer actively maintained by their contributors.

PicketLink

PicketLink was an umbrella for several security-related projects in the Red Hat/JBoss Middleware ecosystem. While Agorava was never an official JBoss project, it was created for its ecosystem and standards like CDI. Therefore, supporting OAuth and Java EE Security through the means of PicketLink seemed a logical step for Agorava.

PicketLink is an Application Security Framework for Java EE applications. It provided features for authenticating users, authorizing access to business methods of your application, managing the application's users, groups, roles, and permissions, etc.

These are the top eight Java Application Security problems solved by PicketLink:

1. What's the best way to add security to the application?

2. How do I authenticate and authorize users?

3. How can I control access to classes and methods?

4. How do I add Identity and Access Management (IAM) to my application?

5. How can I create a secure multitenancy architecture for my SaaS (Software as a Service) application?

6. How can I enable Single Sign-On based on SAML (Security Assertion Markup Language) in my application?

7. How do I add authentication and authorization to my REST layer and API?

8. How can my application authenticate users using their Facebook, Twitter, or Google accounts?

Figure 5-12 shows an overview of PicketLink, its key components, and technologies it supports. Some marked "Coming Soon" were still under development and did not come with the GA (Generally Available or "Stable") versions of PicketLink.

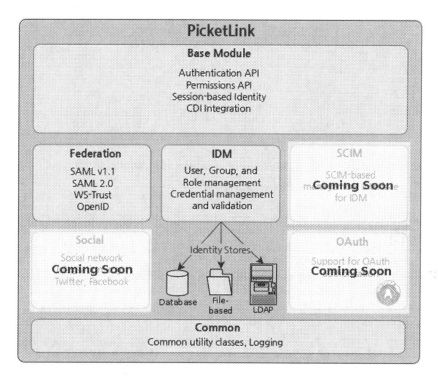

Figure 5-12. *PicketLink Overview*

Agorava does, however, use mainly base functionality of PicketLink, like Authentication API or CDI Integration, adding specialized OAuth and social connectivity of its own.

The "dance" through the authentication flow is conducted by the PicketLink element Authenticator. Here is an example of how to extend `BaseAuthenticator`:

```
@PicketLink
public class SimpleAuthenticator extends BaseAuthenticator {
    @Inject DefaultLoginCredentials credentials;
    @Override
    public void authenticate() {
        if ("agentsmith".equals(credentials.getUserId()) &&
            "matrix123".equals(credentials.getPassword())) {
            setStatus(AuthenticationStatus.SUCCESS);
            setAccount(new User("agentsmith"));
        } else {
            setStatus(AuthenticationStatus.FAILURE);
```

```
        FacesContext.getCurrentInstance().addMessage(null, new
FacesMessage("Authentication Failure - The username or password you
provided were invalid."));
      }
    }
}
```

"Agorava PicketLink" in the next chapter will show in more detail how PicketLink is applied by Agorava Core and its PicketLink module.

SocialAuth

SocialAuth was an authentication library for Java and Android.

Its features include the following:

- Authentication

  - Through external OAuth providers like Gmail, Hotmail, Yahoo, Twitter, Facebook, LinkedIn, Foursquare, Myspace, Salesforce, Yammer, Google Plus, and Instagram

  - Through OpenID providers

- Easy user registration

- Importing contacts from networking sites

Here's an example for a status update using SocialAuth via CDI:

```
@RequestScoped
@Named("socialAuthUpdateStatus")
public class UpdateStatus implements Serializable {
    private static final Logger log = Logger.
    getLogger(UpdateStatus.class);
    @Inject
    SocialAuth socialauth;

    String statusText;
    /**
     * Method which updates the status on profile.
     *
```

```
 * @param ActionEvent
 * @throws Exception
 */
public void updateStatus() throws Exception {
     final HttpServletRequest request = (HttpServletRequest)
     FacesContext
                 .getCurrentInstance().getExternalContext().
                 getRequest();
     String statusText = request.getParameter("statusMessage");
     if (statusText != null && !statusText.equals("")) {
          socialauth.setStatus(statusText);
          socialauth.updateStatus();
          setStatus("Status Updated Successfully");
          System.out.println("status text:" + statusText);
     }
}
public String getStatus() {
     return statusText;
}
public void setStatus(String statusText) {
     this.statusText = statusText;
}
}
```

OACC

OACC, pronounced "oak" (like the original code name of Java), was a Java API to both enforce and manage your application's authentication and authorization needs. OACC provides permission-based authorization services to enforce application security.

Its features include

- Authentication

- Identity delegation

- Data store

- Permission-based security model

- Authorization

- RBAC modeling

- Permission delegation

- Multitenancy

- Caching

Here's an example application:

```
public class OACCSampleApplication {
    public static void main(String[] args) throws Exception {
        // get a connection to the oacc database
        String url = "jdbc:postgresql://localhost/oaccdb?user=oaccuser&
        password=oaccpwd";

        try (Connection con = DriverManager.getConnection(url)) {
            // get the access control context
            AccessControlContext accessControlContext =
SQLAccessControlContextFactory.getAccessControlContext(con,
"OACC",
SQLProfile.PostgreSQL_9_3_RECURSIVE,
BCryptPasswordEncryptor.newInstance(12));
            // create new admin
            createAdmin(accessControlContext);
            // create new user
            createUser(accessControlContext);
            // login as admin
            loginAdmin(accessControlContext, "adminJoe", "pa55wOrd");
            // attempt to update user while logged in as admin
            updateUser(accessControlContext, "jsmith");
        }
    }
    private static void createAdmin(AccessControlContext
    accessControlContext) {
        // authenticate as the system resource (the super user) to set up an
        initial admin
```

```
    accessControlContext.authenticate(Resources.getInstance(0),
    PasswordCredentials.newInstance("yourOaccSystemPassword".
    toCharArray()));
    // persist the admin in your application for example:
    AppAdmin admin = new AppAdmin.Builder()
            .login("adminJoe")
            .email("joeBloe@company.com")
            .build().create();
    // create the corresponding OACC resource
    final Resource adminResource
            = accessControlContext.createResource("ADMIN",
            "APP_DOMAIN", admin.getLogin(),
            PasswordCredentials.newInstance("pa55wOrd".toCharArray()));
    System.out.println("created new ADMIN resource with Id=" +
    adminResource.getId());
    // grant permissions to query about, view and deactivate any user
    account, but not to edit it
Set<ResourcePermission> permissions = new HashSet<>();
    permissions.add(ResourcePermissions.getInstance(ResourcePermissions.
    QUERY));        permissions.add(ResourcePermissions.
    getInstance("VIEW"));        permissions.add(ResourcePermissions.
    getInstance("DEACTIVATE"));

    accessControlContext.setGlobalResourcePermissions(adminResource,
    "USER", "APP_DOMAIN", permissions);
    accessControlContext.unauthenticate();
    }
    private static void createUser(AccessControlContext
    accessControlContext) {
    // persist the user in your application
    // e.g. UserHOME.create("jsmith", "Jane", "Smith", "jsmith@mail.com",
    userResource.getId())
    // for example:
    AppUser user = new AppUser.Builder()
            .login("jsmith")
            .firstName("Jane").lastName("Smith")
```

```
        .email("jsmith@mail.com")
        .build().create();
    // don't have to be authenticated to create users because the
    resource class has the unauthenticatedCreateAllowed-flag set
    final Resource userResource
        = accessControlContext.createResource("USER",
        "APP_DOMAIN", user.getLogin(),
        PasswordCredentials.newInstance("pa$$word1".toCharArray()));
    System.out.println("created new USER resource with Id=" +
    userResource.getId());
}
private static void loginAdmin(AccessControlContext
accessControlContext, String adminLogin,  String password) {
    // authenticate as the admin resource        accessControlContext.
    authenticate(Resources.getInstance(adminLogin),
    PasswordCredentials.newInstance(password.toCharArray()));
}
private static void updateUser(AccessControlContext
accessControlContext, String userLogin) {
    // assert that the authenticated admin has VIEW permission *before*
    attempting to load the user        accessControlContext.assertResourceP
    ermissions(accessControlContext.getSessionResource(), Resources.getIn
    stance(userLogin),
    ResourcePermissions.getInstance("VIEW"));
    // load the user information and modify the local copy
    AppUser user = new AppUser.Finder().findByLogin(userLogin);
    user.setEmail("other@mail.com");
    // assert that the authenticated admin has EDIT permission *before*
    attempting to save the user        accessControlContext.assertResourceP
    ermissions(accessControlContext.getSessionResource(),
    Resources.getInstance(userLogin),
    ResourcePermissions.getInstance("EDIT"));
    // save the user
```

```
    // !NOTE! we won't get here because adminResource doesn't have EDIT
    permission on the userResource
    user.save();
    }
}
```

Summary

Following an overview of security in social media and relevant security standards in the previous chapter, we learned about important security frameworks for the Java platform and how to use them with social networks in this chapter.

## CHAPTER 6

Social Frameworks

The previous chapter dealt with security frameworks like Soteria, Keycloak, or Spring Security. In this chapter, we'll take a look at social frameworks like Meta Business SDK, Twitter4J, Twitter API Client, Legacy frameworks like Agorava, Spring Social, or Facebook4J as well as frameworks for special purposes or vertical social networks.

Meta

Meta Platforms owns a variety of social products:

- Facebook

- Instagram

- (Facebook) Messenger

- WhatsApp

- Threads

- VR products like Horizon Worlds

The combined user base is the largest of any social net. More than 200 million businesses use Facebook, and more than 7 million advertisers actively promote their business on Facebook/Meta.

Enough reason, that unlike some other big social networks, Meta offers a number of SDKs including dedicated business SDKs and support for a large variety of programming languages itself.

© Werner Keil 2024
W. Keil, *Enterprise Social for the Java Platform*, https://doi.org/10.1007/978-1-4842-9571-7_6

The two most active Java Business APIs for Meta are as follows:

- Meta Business SDK – The official Business SDK suite by Meta

- WhatsApp Business Java API SDK – A community-driven WhatsApp Business SDK for Java. Currently superior to the official Meta SDKs for WhatsApp using Java, because they do not offer a strong Java object model yet

Meta Business SDK

The Meta Business SDK [36] provides access to various Meta business APIs. It is an evolution of the Facebook Marketing API SDK, including the Marketing API and other Meta APIs like Pages, Business Manager, Instagram, etc., allowing to build customized enterprise solutions that seamlessly integrate a range of Meta services.

Overview

The Meta Business SDK consists of the following parts:

- Business Manager API – Allows to manage Meta assets, permissions, and ad campaigns for Facebook pages and ad accounts

- Pages API – Allows to manage a business presence and community on Facebook

- Marketing API – Allows to manage ad products, create, edit, or delete ads, and analyze their performance

- Instagram Graph API – Allows to manage an enterprise presence on Instagram

Where's WhatsApp?
While WhatsApp (Meta) Business accounts exist for enterprises, WhatsApp support is currently not part of the Meta Business SDK.

The API support for Java and other languages is currently more rudimentary than that for other Meta services through the Business SDK. It's mostly down to REST/ HTTP client calls from the language of your choice. We'll show a WhatsApp example for Java here, but a more convenient Java wrapper by the community exists in the form of WhatsApp Business Java API SDK.

Smoke Test

These steps explain how to install the Meta Business SDK for Java using Maven and test the installation.

Prerequisites

You need the following:

- A Meta Developer Account

- A Meta app registered on `https://developers.facebook.com/`

- Your app secret

- An access token

- An Ad Account

Follow these steps to install the SDK and test your application:

1. After creating a Maven project with the IDE of your choice, add the following dependency to your `pom.xml` file:

```
<!-- https://mvnrepository.com/artifact/com.facebook.business.
sdk/facebook-java-business-sdk -->
<dependency>
<groupId>com.facebook.business.sdk</groupId>
  <artifactId>facebook-java-business-sdk</artifactId>
  <version>[8.0.3,)</version>
</dependency>
```

2. Create a Java class called something like `SmokeTestFBJavaSDK`, and add the following code. Note that {access-token}, {appsecret}, and {adaccount-id} are placeholders for your actual values. Make sure to externalize them appropriately, especially if you share them with others:

```
import com.facebook.ads.sdk.APIContext;
import com.facebook.ads.sdk.APINodeList;
import com.facebook.ads.sdk.AdAccount;
import com.facebook.ads.sdk.Campaign;
```

```
public class SmokeTestFBJavaSDK
{
    public static final APIContext context = new APIContext(
            "{access-token}",
            "{appsecret}"
    );
    public static void main(String[] args)
    {
        AdAccount account = new AdAccount("act_{{adaccount-id}}",
        context);
        try {
            APINodeList<Campaign> campaigns = account.
            getCampaigns().requestAllFields().execute();
            for(Campaign campaign : campaigns) {
                System.out.println(campaign.getFieldName());
            }
        } catch (Exception e) {
            e.printStackTrace();
        }
    }}
```

3. Build and run your application. You should see the output in the console. If there's an error about an expired token, please request a new access token, for example, by using the refresh token and try again.

Examples

Here are code examples for selected business use cases.

Ads Buying

The following examples show how to create ad campaigns for Click-to-Messenger Ads and Facebook page promotions.

Click-to-Messenger Ads allow people to directly start a thread with your Facebook page when they click on your ad.

You need an Ad Account ID.

This example shows you how to create an ad that will run during a designated time period:

```
AdSet adSet = new AdAccount(act_<AD_ACCOUNT_ID>, context).createAdSet()
  .setName("My Ad Set")
  .setOptimizationGoal(AdSet.EnumOptimizationGoal.VALUE_REACH)
  .setBillingEvent(AdSet.EnumBillingEvent.VALUE_IMPRESSIONS)
  .setBidAmount(2L)
  .setDailyBudget(1000L)
  .setCampaignId(<CAMPAIGN_ID>)
  .setTargeting(
    new Targeting()
      .setFieldGeoLocations(
        new TargetingGeoLocation()
          .setFieldCountries(Arrays.asList("US"))
      )
  )
  .setStartTime(start_time)
  .setEndTime(end_time)
  .setStatus(AdSet.EnumStatus.VALUE_PAUSED)
  .execute();
String ad_set_id = adSet.getId();
```

Create an ad to increase traffic to your Facebook page by promoting it. You need

- An Ad Account ID

- A Facebook Page ID

The following example shows how to create an ad campaign promoting your Page to get more likes. The ad will run in the United States with a daily budget of 1000 USD with the goal of ad impressions:

```
Campaign campaign = new AdAccount(<ACCOUNT_ID>, context).createCampaign()
  .setObjective(Campaign.EnumObjective.VALUE_PAGE_LIKES)
  .setStatus(Campaign.EnumStatus.VALUE_PAUSED)
  .setBuyingType("AUCTION")
  .setName("My Campaign")
```

```
  .execute();
String campaign_id = campaign.getId();
AdSet adSet = new AdAccount(<ACCOUNT_ID>, context).createAdSet()
  .setStatus(AdSet.EnumStatus.VALUE_PAUSED)
  .setTargeting(
    new Targeting()
      .setFieldGeoLocations(
        new TargetingGeoLocation()
          .setFieldCountries(Arrays.asList("US"))
      )
  )
  .setDailyBudget(1000L)
  .setBillingEvent(AdSet.EnumBillingEvent.VALUE_IMPRESSIONS)
  .setBidAmount(20L)
  .setCampaignId(campaign_id)
  .setOptimizationGoal(AdSet.EnumOptimizationGoal.VALUE_PAGE_LIKES)
  .setPromotedObject("{\"page_id\": \"" + <PAGE_ID> + "\"}")
  .setName("My AdSet")
  .execute();
String ad_set_id = adSet.getId();
AdCreative creative = new AdAccount(<ACCOUNT_ID>, context).
createAdCreative()
  .setBody("Like My Page")
  .setImageUrl("https://static.xx.fbcdn.net/rsrc.php/v3/yu/
r/66zXtGTxCWr.png")
  .setName("My Creative")
  .setObjectId(<PAGE_ID>)
  .setTitle("My Page Like Ad")
  .execute();
String creative_id = creative.getId();
Ad ad = new AdAccount(<ACCOUNT_ID>, context).createAd()
  .setStatus (Ad.EnumStatus.VALUE_PAUSED)
  .setAdsetId(ad_set_id)
  .setName("My Ad")
  .setCreative(
```

```
  new AdCreative()
    .setFieldId(creative_id)
)
.setParam("ad_format", "DESKTOP_FEED_STANDARD")
.execute();
String ad_id = ad.getId();
APINodeList<AdPreview> adPreviews = new Ad(ad_id, context).getPreviews()
  .setAdFormat(AdPreview.EnumAdFormat.VALUE_DESKTOP_FEED_STANDARD)
  .execute();
```

Batch Mode

Meta APIs offer a Batch Mode, somewhat similar to Jakarta Batch or Spring Batch, allowing to send a single HTTP request that contains multiple Facebook Graph API calls. Independent operations are processed in parallel, while dependent operations are processed sequentially. Once all operations are complete, a consolidated response is passed back to the caller and the connection is closed.

This is an example for the Batch Mode:

```
BatchRequest batch = new BatchRequest(context);
account.createCampaign()
  .setName("Meta Java SDK Batch Test Campaign")
  .setObjective(Campaign.EnumObjective.VALUE_LINK_CLICKS)
  .setSpendCap(10000L)
  .setStatus(Campaign.EnumStatus.VALUE_PAUSED)
  .addToBatch(batch, "campaignRequest");
account.createAdSet()
  .setName("Meta Java SDK Batch Test AdSet")
  .setCampaignId("{result=campaignRequest:$.id}")
  .setStatus(AdSet.EnumStatus.VALUE_PAUSED)
  .setBillingEvent(AdSet.EnumBillingEvent.VALUE_IMPRESSIONS)
  .setDailyBudget(1000L)
  .setBidAmount(100L)
  .setOptimizationGoal(AdSet.EnumOptimizationGoal.VALUE_IMPRESSIONS)
  .setTargeting(targeting)
  .addToBatch(batch, "adsetRequest");
```

```
account.createAdImage()
  .addUploadFile("file", imageFile)
  .addToBatch(batch, "imageRequest");
account.createAdCreative()
  .setTitle("Java SDK Batch Test Creative")
  .setBody("Java SDK Batch Test Creative")
  .setImageHash("{result=imageRequest:$.images.*.hash}")
  .setLinkUrl("www.facebook.com")
  .setObjectUrl("www.facebook.com")
  .addToBatch(batch, "creativeRequest");
account.createAd()
  .setName("Meta Java SDK Batch Test ad")
  .setAdsetId("{result=adsetRequest:$.id}")
  .setCreative("{creative_id:{result=creativeRequest:$.id}}")
  .setStatus("PAUSED")
  .setBidAmount(100L)
  .addToBatch(batch);
List<APIResponse> responses = batch.execute();
// responses contains the result of each API call in order. However,
if the API calls have dependency, then some result could be null.
```

Instagram

Manage comments on Instagram using the Meta Business SDK.

You need

- An Instagram Professional Account ID

- Facebook Page ID of the Page linked to an Instagram Professional Account

- Your Meta App ID

- A Page access token of the Page linked to your Instagram Professional Account

The following example comments on your media objects, analyzes these comments, filters against specific criteria, and replies to comments matching those criteria.

1. Use the /media/comments endpoint to get all comments and their IDs.

2. Select the comment you want to reply to and use its comment ID to reply to the user.

```
context = new APIContext(page_access_token_for_ig).
enableDebug(false);
APINodeList<IGComment> igComments = new IGMedia(<IG_POST_ID>,
context).getComments()
   .execute();
String ig_comment_id = igComments.get(0).getId();
IGComment igComment = new IGComment(ig_comment_id, context).get()
   .execute();
APINodeList<IGComment> igCommentRepliess = new IGComment(ig_
comment_id, context).getReplies()
   .execute();
```

WhatsApp

This example adds functionality to send WhatsApp messages via the API from a Java app. You need

- A Java IDE of your choice.

- Ensure to have Java 11 or higher.

- Register at Meta for Developers.

- Enable two-factor authentication for your account.

- Ensure your developer account is linked to a Meta Business account.

Create an app on Meta for Developers. Select *My Apps*, then click *Create App*, and select *Business* as the app type.

The example code will look like this:

```
import java.io.IOException;
import java.net.URI;
import java.net.URISyntaxException;
import java.net.http.HttpClient;
import java.net.http.HttpRequest;
```

```java
import java.net.http.HttpResponse;
import java.net.http.HttpResponse.BodyHandlers;

public class App
{
    public static void main( String[] args )
    {
        try {
            HttpRequest request = HttpRequest.newBuilder()
                .uri(new URI("https://graph.facebook.com/v13.0/<YOUR PHONE
                NUMBER ID>/messages"))
                .header("Authorization", "Bearer <YOUR BEARER TOKEN>")
                .header("Content-Type", "application/json")
                .POST(HttpRequest.BodyPublishers.ofString("{ \"messaging_
                product\": \"whatsapp\", \"recipient_type\": \"individual\",
                \"to\": \"<TARGET PHONE NUMBER>\", \"type\": \"template\",
                \"template\": { \"name\": \"hello_world\", \"language\": {
                \"code\": \"en_US\" } } }"))
                .build();
            HttpClient http = HttpClient.newHttpClient();
            HttpResponse<String> response = http.send(request,BodyHandlers.
            ofString());
            System.out.println(response.body());

        } catch (URISyntaxException | IOException |
        InterruptedException e) {
            e.printStackTrace();
        }
    }
}
```

WhatsApp Business Java API SDK

WhatsApp Business Java API SDK [59] is a Java API developed by Mauricio Binda da Costa. It implements the official WhatsApp Cloud API and WhatsApp Business Management API, allowing your application to

- Manage your WhatsApp Business Account assets, like message templates and phone numbers

- Send messages to your contacts, like text messages, messages with buttons, videos, images, stickers, etc.

- Upload, delete, and retrieve media files

- Receive webhook events

While it only started in December 2022 and the README claims it is still under construction, there are regular updates and version releases almost every month, so despite not being an official Meta SDK, it still makes a solid impression.

The library and examples require Java 17 or above.

Installation

Add the JitPack repository to your Maven POM file:

```
<repositories>
    <repository>
        <id>jitpack.io</id>
        <url>https://jitpack.io</url>
    </repository>
</repositories>
```

Add the following Maven dependency to your POM file:

```
<dependency>
    <groupId>com.github.Bindambc</groupId>
    <artifactId>whatsapp-business-java-api</artifactId>
    <version>v0.3.3</version>
</dependency>
```

v0.3.3 is currently the latest version, adjusted to newer versions where available.

Examples

Sending a simple text message:

```
WhatsappApiFactory factory = WhatsappApiFactory.
newInstance(TestUtils.TOKEN);
WhatsappBusinessCloudApi whatsappBusinessCloudApi = factory.
newBusinessCloudApi();
        var message = MessageBuilder.builder()//
                .setTo(PHONE_NUMBER_1)//
                .buildTextMessage(new TextMessage()//
            .setBody(Formatter.bold("Hello world!") + "\nSome code here:
            \n" + Formatter.code("hello world code here"))//
                .setPreviewUrl(false));
        whatsappBusinessCloudApi.sendMessage(PHONE_NUMBER_ID, message);
```

Sending a message with buttons (template):

```
WhatsappApiFactory factory = WhatsappApiFactory.
newInstance(TestConstants.TOKEN);
WhatsappBusinessCloudApi whatsappBusinessCloudApi = factory.
newBusinessCloudApi();
        var message = MessageBuilder.builder()//
                .setTo(PHONE_NUMBER_1)//
                .buildTemplateMessage(//
                    new TemplateMessage()//
                        .setLanguage(new Language(LanguageType.
                        PT_BR))//
                        .setName("schedule_confirmation3")//
  .addComponent(//
    new Component(ComponentType.BODY)//
                                        .addParameter(new
                                        TextParameter("Mauricio"))//
                                        .addParameter(new
                                        TextParameter("04/11/2022"))//
                                        .addParameter(new
                                        TextParameter("14:30")))//
                );
whatsappBusinessCloudApi.sendMessage(PHONE_NUMBER_ID, message);
```

Sending a message with a list:

```
WhatsappApiFactory factory = WhatsappApiFactory.
newInstance(TestUtils.TOKEN);
WhatsappBusinessCloudApi whatsappBusinessCloudApi = factory.
newBusinessCloudApi();
        var message = MessageBuilder.builder()//
                .setTo(PHONE_NUMBER_1)//
                .buildInteractiveMessage(InteractiveMessage.build() //
          .setAction(new Action() //
                .setButtonText("BUTTON_TEXT") //
                .addSection(new Section() //
                   .setTitle("Title 1") //
                    .addRow(new Row() //
.setId("SECTION_1_ROW_1_ID") //
.setTitle("Title 1") //
.setDescription("SECTION_1_ROW_1_DESCRIPTION")) //
.addRow(new Row() //
.setId("SECTION_1_ROW_2_ID") //
.setTitle("Title 2") //
.setDescription("SECTION_1_ROW_2_DESCRIPTION")) //
.addRow(new Row() //
.setId("SECTION_1_ROW_3_ID") //
.setTitle("Title 3") //
.setDescription("SECTION_1_ROW_3_DESCRIPTION")) //
) //
 .addSection(new Section() //
     .setTitle("Title 2") //
.addRow(new Row() //
.setId("SECTION_2_ROW_1_ID") //
.setTitle("Title 1") //
.setDescription("SECTION_2_ROW_1_DESCRIPTION")) //
.addRow(new Row() //
.setId("SECTION_2_ROW_2_ID") //
.setTitle("Title 2") //
.setDescription("SECTION_2_ROW_2_DESCRIPTION")) //
```

```
.addRow(new Row() //
.setId("SECTION_2_ROW_3_ID") //
.setTitle("Title 3") //
.setDescription("SECTION_2_ROW_3_DESCRIPTION")) //
                        )
                ) //
        .setType(InteractiveMessageType.LIST) //
        .setHeader(new Header() //
        .setType(HeaderType.TEXT) //
        .setText("Header Text")) //
        .setBody(new Body() //
          .setText("Body message")) //
            .setFooter(new Footer() //
            .setText("Footer Text")) //
        );
    MessageResponse messageResponse = whatsappBusinessCloudApi.
    sendMessage(PHONE_NUMBER_ID, message);
System.out.println(messageResponse);
```

Sending a message with a contact:

```
WhatsappApiFactory factory = WhatsappApiFactory.newInstance(TestUtils.TOKEN);
WhatsappBusinessCloudApi whatsappBusinessCloudApi = factory.
newBusinessCloudApi();
    var message = MessageBuilder.builder()//
            .setTo(PHONE_NUMBER_1)//
            .buildContactMessage(new ContactMessage()//
                .addContacts(new ContactsItem()//
                    .addPhones(new PhonesItem()//
                        .setPhone(PHONE_NUMBER_1)//
                        .setType(AddressType.HOME))//
                    .setName(new Name()//
                        .setFormattedName("Mauricio Binda")//
                        .setFirstName("Mauricio"))//
                ));
    whatsappBusinessCloudApi.sendMessage(PHONE_NUMBER_ID, message);
```

Sending an audio message:

```
WhatsappApiFactory factory = WhatsappApiFactory.newInstance(TOKEN);
WhatsappBusinessCloudApi whatsappBusinessCloudApi = factory.
newBusinessCloudApi();
            var audioMessage = new AudioMessage()//
            .setId("6418001414900549");
            var message = MessageBuilder.builder()//
            .setTo(PHONE_NUMBER_1)//
            .buildAudioMessage(audioMessage);
            MessageResponse messageResponse = whatsappBusinessCloudApi.
            sendMessage(PHONE_NUMBER_ID, message);
```

Sending a video message:

```
WhatsappApiFactory factory = WhatsappApiFactory.newInstance(TOKEN);
WhatsappBusinessCloudApi whatsappBusinessCloudApi = factory.
newBusinessCloudApi();
            var videoMessage = new VideoMessage()//
            .setId("1236364143659727")// media id (uploaded before)
            .setCaption("See this video");
            var message = MessageBuilder.builder()//
            .setTo(PHONE_NUMBER_1)//
            .buildVideoMessage(videoMessage);
            MessageResponse messageResponse = whatsappBusinessCloudApi.
            sendMessage(PHONE_NUMBER_ID, message);
```

Webhooks

Webhooks are triggered when a user performs an action or the status for a message sent by a business changes.

Here's an example:

```
//payload = the webhook payload json sent by Whatsapp
//using WebHook.constructEvent() to deserialize event
WebHookEvent event = WebHook.constructEvent(payload);
```

Mastodon

There are three Java clients for Mastodon according to the website, but only BigBone seems reasonably active.

BigBone

BigBone is a fork of the Mastodon4J project, a client library for Java and Kotlin.

Overview

The main features of BigBone are as follows:

- Act on statuses on your timelines

  - Home

  - Local

  - Federated

- Post new statuses or edit existing ones (including media uploads)

- Favorite and bookmark statuses

- Manage lists

- Post polls or vote on them

- Schedule statuses

- Send direct messages to other people

- Manage filters

- Follow/unfollow hashtags

Installation

Add the following to the Maven POM of your project.

Snapshot Repository

```
<repositories>
    <repository>
        <id>maven-central-snapshots</id>
```

```
    <name>Maven Central Snapshot Repository</name>
    <url>https://s01.oss.sonatype.org/content/repositories/
    snapshots/</url>
    <releases>
        <enabled>false</enabled>
    </releases>
    <snapshots>
        <enabled>true</enabled>
    </snapshots>
  </repository>
</repositories>
```

Dependencies

```
<dependency>
    <groupId>social.bigbone</groupId>
    <artifactId>bigbone</artifactId>
    <version>2.0.0-SNAPSHOT</version>
</dependency>
<dependency>
    <groupId>social.bigbone</groupId>
    <artifactId>bigbone-rx</artifactId>
    <version>2.0.0-SNAPSHOT</version>
</dependency>
```

Examples

Get an access token

    https://docs.joinmastodon.org/methods/apps/

Get a timeline

```
public class GetPublicTimeline {
    public static void main(final String[] args) throws
    BigBoneRequestException {
        final String instance = args[0];

        // Instantiate client
```

```
        final MastodonClient client = new MastodonClient.Builder(instance)
            .build();

        // Get statuses from public timeline
        final Pageable<Status> statuses = client.timelines().
        getPublicTimeline(LOCAL_AND_REMOTE).execute();
        statuses.getPart().forEach(status -> System.out.println(status.
        getContent()));
    }
}
```

Get instance information

```
public class GetInstanceInfo {
    public static void main(final String[] args) throws
    BigBoneRequestException {
        final String instance = args[0];

        // Instantiate client
        final MastodonClient client = new MastodonClient.Builder(instance)
            .build();

        // Get instance info and dump it to the console as JSON
        final Instance instanceInfo = client.instances().getInstance().
        execute();
        final Gson gson = new Gson();
        System.out.println(gson.toJson(instanceInfo));
    }
}
```

Get bookmarks

```
public class GetBookmarks {
    public static void main(final String[] args) throws
    BigBoneRequestException {
        final String instance = args[0];
        final String accessToken = args[1];

        // Instantiate client
        final MastodonClient client = new MastodonClient.Builder(instance)
```

```
        .accessToken(accessToken)
        .build();

    // Get bookmarks
    final Pageable<Status> bookmarks = client.bookmarks().
    getBookmarks().execute();
    bookmarks.getPart().forEach(bookmark -> {
        String statusText = bookmark.getContent() + "\n";
        System.out.print(statusText);
    });
    }
}
```

Perform a simple search

```
public class PerformSimpleSearch {
    public static void main(final String[] args) throws
    BigBoneRequestException {
        final String instance = args[0];
        final String accessToken = args[1];
        final String searchTerm = args[2];

        // Instantiate client
        final MastodonClient client = new MastodonClient.Builder(instance)
            .accessToken(accessToken)
            .build();

        // Perform search and print results
        final Search searchResult = client.search().
        searchContent(searchTerm).execute();
        searchResult.getAccounts().forEach(account -> System.out.
        println(account.getDisplayName()));
        searchResult.getStatuses().forEach(status -> System.out.
        println(status.getContent()));
        searchResult.getHashtags().forEach(hashtag -> System.out.
        println(hashtag.getName()));
    }
}
```

Twitter/X

The social network formerly known as Twitter has at least two Java clients with an object model wrapped around the Twitter/X REST APIs.

Twitter API Client

In August 2021, Twitter started its own API Client Library for Java [35]. Quite late, also given Twitter had been an active participant in the JCP [11] and host to several JCP EC F2F meetings in the Bay Area, but supporting the Twitter v2 API only, it seemed a measure to convince developers into migrating to the new API. The GitHub repo still says "This SDK is in beta and is not ready for production", and there was only contribution by three committers; all seem to have left the company shortly before or after the Elon Musk takeover.

Installation

Add this dependency to your project's POM:

```
<dependency>
  <groupId>com.twitter</groupId>
  <artifactId>twitter-api-java-sdk</artifactId>
  <version>2.0.3</version>
</dependency>
```

TWITTER TO X MIGRATION

As Elon Musk rebrands Twitter to X, at some point, even domains like twitter.com or URLs underneath that site could be switched off and no longer work. That may affect some of the settings and steps listed here.

Examples

You must first register a Twitter application to obtain a username and password to access the Twitter API. To register a new application for use with the API Client:

1. Go to `https://dev.twitter.com`

2. Log in and click **Create an app**

3. Click **Add New Application**

4. Under **Application Info**, enter values for the following parameters:

    - Application Name – This is the name of your application that is displayed at the end of each post, for example, your company name.

    - Application Description – Enter a short description of the application.

    - Website – This is the URL to your website, for example, `http://www.mysite.com`.

    - Callback URL – Set this to http://domain/wps/wcmsocial/servlet/oAuthCB/twitter where "domain" is your domain name.

5. Read the terms and conditions and select **I Agree**.

6. Enter the security/captcha information if required.

7. Your Consumer Key and Consumer Secret are displayed. Write them down in a safe place.

8. Click the **Settings** tab.

9. In the **Application Type** section, set the **Access** property to Read and write.

10. Click the **Update this Twitter application's settings**.

API example

```java
public class TwitterApiExample {
  public static void main(String[] args) {
    /**
     * Set the credentials for the required APIs.
     * The Java SDK supports TwitterCredentialsOAuth2 &
       TwitterCredentialsBearer.
     * Check the 'security' tag of the required APIs in https://api.
       twitter.com/2/openapi.json in order
     * to use the right credential object.
     */
    TwitterApi apiInstance = new TwitterApi(new TwitterCredentialsOAuth2(
        System.getenv("TWITTER_OAUTH2_CLIENT_ID"),
        System.getenv("TWITTER_OAUTH2_CLIENT_SECRET"),
        System.getenv("TWITTER_OAUTH2_ACCESS_TOKEN"),
        System.getenv("TWITTER_OAUTH2_REFRESH_TOKEN")));

    Set<String> tweetFields = new HashSet<>();
    tweetFields.add("author_id");
    tweetFields.add("id");
    tweetFields.add("created_at");
    try {
     // findTweetById
     Get2TweetsIdResponse result = apiInstance.tweets().findTweetById("20")
       .tweetFields(tweetFields)
       .execute();
     if(result.getErrors() != null && result.getErrors().size() > 0) {
       System.out.println("Error:");
       result.getErrors().forEach(e -> {
         System.out.println(e.toString());
         if (e instanceof ResourceUnauthorizedProblem) {
           System.out.println(((ResourceUnauthorizedProblem) e).getTitle()
           + " " + ((ResourceUnauthorizedProblem) e).getDetail());
         }
       });
```

```
    } else {
      System.out.println("findTweetById - Tweet Text: " + result.
      toString());
    }
  } catch (ApiException e) {
    System.err.println("Status code: " + e.getCode());
    System.err.println("Reason: " + e.getResponseBody());
    System.err.println("Response headers: " + e.getResponseHeaders());
    e.printStackTrace();
  }
 }
}
```

Get all desired fields

```
Set<String> tweetFields = new HashSet<>();
tweetFields.add("non_public_metrics");
tweetFields.add("promoted_metrics");
tweetFields.add("organic_metrics");
// Get all available fields excluding Tweet Fields 'non_public_
metrics', 'promoted_metrics' & 'organic_metrics'
Get2TweetsIdResponse result = apiInstance.tweets().
findTweetById("20")        .tweetFields(tweetFields).
excludeInputFields().execute();
// Get all the response fields
Get2TweetsIdResponse result2 = apiInstance.tweets().
findTweetById("20").excludeInputFields().execute();
```

HelloWorld example

```
public class HelloWorld {

  public static void main(String[] args) {
    /**
     * Set the credentials for the required APIs.
     * The Java SDK supports TwitterCredentialsOAuth2 &
       TwitterCredentialsBearer.
```

```
 * Check the 'security' tag of the required APIs in https://api.
   twitter.com/2/openapi.json in order
 * to use the right credential object.
 */
TwitterApi apiInstance = new TwitterApi(new
TwitterCredentialsBearer(System.getenv("TWITTER_BEARER_TOKEN")));

Set<String> tweetFields = new HashSet<>();
tweetFields.add("author_id");
tweetFields.add("id");
tweetFields.add("created_at");

try {
 // findTweetById
 Get2TweetsIdResponse result = apiInstance.tweets().findTweetById("20")
  .tweetFields(tweetFields)
  .execute();
 if(result.getErrors() != null && result.getErrors().size() > 0) {
   System.out.println("Error:");

   result.getErrors().forEach(e -> {
     System.out.println(e.toString());
     if (e instanceof ResourceUnauthorizedProblem) {
       System.out.println(((ResourceUnauthorizedProblem) e).getTitle()
       + " " + ((ResourceUnauthorizedProblem) e).getDetail());
     }
   });
 } else {
   System.out.println("findTweetById - Tweet Text: " + result.
   toString());
 }
} catch (ApiException e) {
   System.err.println("Status code: " + e.getCode());
   System.err.println("Reason: " + e.getResponseBody());
   System.err.println("Response headers: " + e.getResponseHeaders());
```

```
      e.printStackTrace();
    }
  }
}
```

HelloWorld example (Streaming)

```java
public class HelloWorldStreaming {

  public static void main(String[] args) {
    /**
     * Set the credentials for the required APIs.
     * The Java SDK supports TwitterCredentialsOAuth2 &
       TwitterCredentialsBearer.
     * Check the 'security' tag of the required APIs in https://api.
       twitter.com/2/openapi.json in order
     * to use the right credential object.
     */
    TwitterApi apiInstance = new TwitterApi(new
    TwitterCredentialsBearer(System.getenv("TWITTER_BEARER_TOKEN")));
    try {
      TweetsStreamListenersExecutor tsle = new
      TweetsStreamListenersExecutor();
      tsle.stream()
          .streamingHandler(new StreamingTweetHandlerImpl(apiInstance))
          .executeListeners();
      while(tsle.getError() == null) {
        try {
          System.out.println("==> sleeping 5 ");
          Thread.sleep(5000);
        } catch (InterruptedException e) {
          e.printStackTrace();
        }
      }
```

```
    if(tsle.getError() != null) {
      System.err.println("==> Ended with error: " + tsle.getError());
    }
  } catch (ApiException e) {
    System.err.println("Status code: " + e.getCode());
    System.err.println("Reason: " + e.getResponseBody());
    System.err.println("Response headers: " + e.getResponseHeaders());
    e.printStackTrace();
  }
 }
}
```

Twitter4J

Twitter4J is an open source Java library for the Twitter API. With Twitter4J, you can easily

- Post a tweet

- Get the timeline of a user

- Get a list of friends and followers of a user

- Get the favorites of a user

- Send and receive direct messages

- Search for tweets

- Use the Twitter Streaming API

History

Its author, Yusuke Yamamoto, used to work for Twitter in 2012.

While he did, he was briefly meant to represent Twitter in the Social JSR Expert Group.

The last version was 4.1.2 in October 2022. After a longer break between 2018 and 2022, it now seems reasonably well maintained again. A risk, however, is that Twitter4J so far only supports Twitter API v1.1 and with the whole Elon Musk situation at Twitter, nobody knows for sure if and how long both will be available. On the other hand, with Twitter's workforce decimated to just a mere shadow of pre-Musk times, it is unlikely all

services are going to be migrated to v2 only in just a few weeks. And with a Premium v1.1
API offering some revenue, it isn't likely going away overnight without granting paying
users a time to migrate to v2 equivalents. While Gnip has been purchased by Twitter
nearly ten years ago, the Enterprise API was only rebranded from Gnip 2.0 very recently,
and that process may also be hampered by all the developers with experience Musk
either fired or made leave Twitter on their own.

Examples

Get a timeline

```
import twitter4j.Twitter;
import twitter4j.TwitterException;
import twitter4j.v1.Status;

import java.util.List;

class Main {
    public static void main(String[] args) throws TwitterException {
        Twitter twitter = Twitter.getInstance();
        List<Status> statuses = twitter.v1().timelines().getHomeTimeline();
        System.out.println("Showing home timeline.");
        for (Status status : statuses) {
            System.out.println(status.getUser().getName() + ":" +
                    status.getText());
        }
    }
}
```

Post a tweet

```
import twitter4j.Twitter;

Twitter twitter = Twitter.getInstance();
Status status = twitter.v1().tweets().updateStatus(latestStatus);
System.out.println("Successfully updated the status to [" + status.
getText() + "].");
```

Search for tweets

```java
import twitter4j.Twitter;
import twitter4j.TwitterException;
import twitter4j.v1.Query;
import twitter4j.v1.QueryResult;
import twitter4j.v1.Status;

class Main {
    public static void main(String[] args) throws TwitterException {
        Twitter twitter = Twitter.getInstance();
        Query query = Query.of("source:twitter4j yusukey");
        QueryResult result = twitter.v1().search().search(query);
        for (Status status : result.getTweets()) {
            System.out.println("@" + status.getUser().getScreenName() + ":"
            + status.getText());
        }
    }
}
```

Exchange direct messages

```java
import twitter4j.Twitter;
import twitter4j.TwitterException;
import twitter4j.v1.DirectMessage;

class Main {
    public static void main(String[] args) throws TwitterException {
        long recipientId = Long.parseLong(args[0]);
        String message = args[1];
        Twitter twitter = Twitter.getInstance();
        DirectMessage directMessage = twitter.v1().directMessages().
        sendDirectMessage(recipientId, message);
        System.out.printf("Sent: %s to @%d%n", directMessage.getText(),
        directMessage.getRecipientId());
    }
}
```

Streaming API

```java
import twitter4j.*;
import twitter4j.v1.*;
import java.io.IOException;

class Main {
    public static void main(String[] args) throws TwitterException,
IOException {
        StatusListener listener = new StatusListener(){
            @Override
            public void onStatus(Status status) {
                System.out.println("%s : %s".formatted(status.getUser().
                getName(), status.getText()));
            }
            @Override
            public void onDeletionNotice(StatusDeletionNotice
            statusDeletionNotice) {}
            @Override
            public void onTrackLimitationNotice(int numberOfLimitedStatuses) {}
            @Override
            public void onScrubGeo(long userId, long upToStatusId) {}

            @Override
            public void onStallWarning(StallWarning warning) {}
            @Override
            public void onException(Exception ex) {
                ex.printStackTrace();
            }
        };
        TwitterStream twitterStream = Twitter.newBuilder()
                .listener(listener).build().v1().stream();
        // sample() method internally creates a thread which manipulates
        TwitterStream and calls these adequate listener methods continuously.
        twitterStream.sample();
    }
}
```

Specialized Frameworks

The following frameworks allow you to interact with popular specialized social networks using Java or other JVM languages like Kotlin or Groovy for some of them.

Echobox LinkedIn SDK

ebx-linkedin-sdk is a LinkedIn Java client maintained by Echobox, a company offering social media and online marketing solutions particularly for the publishing and media industry.

Installation

Add the following dependency to the Maven POM of your project:

```
<dependency>
  <groupId>com.echobox</groupId>
  <artifactId>ebx-linkedin-sdk</artifactId>
  <version>x.x.x</version>
</dependency>
```

The latest version is currently 4.5.0.

If you enable snapshot repositories in your POM you could also use the latest snapshot version:

```
<repositories>
   <repository>
       <id>oss.sonatype.org-snapshot</id>
       <url>http://oss.sonatype.org/content/repositories/snapshots</url>
       <releases><enabled>false</enabled></releases>
       <snapshots><enabled>true</enabled></snapshots>
   </repository>
</repositories>
```

Usage and Examples

Get LinkedIn credentials:

1. Go to www.linkedin.com/developers/apps.

2. Sign in if you're not logged in yet.

3. Click **Create app**.

4. If you already have a **Company Page**, either select an existing company or select **New Company** and enter the company information.

5. Under **Create an app**, enter values for the following parameters:

   - App name – This is the name of your application displayed at the end of each post, for example, "ApressBookDemoApp", or your company name.

   - LinkedIn page – This is the **Company Page** you created earlier, for example, https://linkedin.com/company/123456.

   - Privacy policy URL – Link to your privacy policy (optional), for example, http://www.mysite.com/privacy.

   - App logo – The logo is displayed to users when they authorize with your app, ideally a square image.

   - Legal agreement – Check that you have read and agree to these terms.

6. Click on **Create app**.

7. In the **Auth** tab, you'll find the **Application credentials** API Key and Client Secret. Click the "Eye" button to reveal the client secret. Record these values.

8. Under **OAuth 2.0 settings**, add a redirect URL for your app, for example, http://localhost:8080/callback.

Request an authorization code:

1. If it is a first-time request, the permission request timed out, or was manually revoked by the member: the browser is redirected to LinkedIn's authorization consent window.

2. If there is an existing permission grant from the member: the authorization screen is bypassed and the member is immediately redirected to the URL provided in the `redirect_uri` query parameter.

3. When the member completes the authorization process, the browser is redirected to the URL provided in the `redirect_uri` query parameter.

```
GET https://www.linkedin.com/oauth/v2/authorization
```

Table 6-1. *Parameters for Authorization Call*

Parameter	Type	Description	Required
response_type	string	The value of this field should always be code	Yes
client_id	string	The API Key value generated when you registered your application	Yes
redirect_uri	url	The URI your users are sent back to after authorization. This value must match one of the redirect URLs defined in your application configuration. For example, `http://localhost:8080/callback`	Yes
state	string	A unique string value of your choice that is hard to guess. Used to prevent CSRF. For example, `state=DCEeFWf45A53sdfKef424`	No
scope	string	URL-encoded, space-delimited list of member permissions your application is requesting on behalf of the user. These must be explicitly requested. For example, `scope=r_liteprofile%20r_emailaddress%20w_member_social`	Yes

Sample request:

```
GET https://www.linkedin.com/oauth/v2/authorization?response_
type=code&client_id={your_client_id}&redirect_uri={your_callback_
url}&state=foobar&scope=r_liteprofile%20r_emailaddress%20w_member_social
```

Use the authorization code to get the access token:

```
VersionedLinkedInClient client = new DefaultVersionedLinkedInClient(Versi
on.DEFAULT_VERSION);
LinkedInClient.AccessToken accessToken = client.
obtainUserAccessToken(clientId, clientSecret, redirectURI, code);
```

Create a LinkedIn Share:

```
VersionedPostConnection postConnection =
    new VersionedPostConnection(new DefaultLinkedInClient(authToken));
Distribution distribution = new Distribution(Distribution.FeedDistribution.
MAIN_FEED);
String commentary = "Message here"
Post post = new Post(ownerURN, commentary, distribution, Post.
LifecycleState.PUBLISHED,
    Post.Visibility.PUBLIC);
String articleLink = "https://www.example.com/1234";
String title = "title";
String description = "description";
PostUtils.fillArticleContent(post, articleLink, imageURN, title,
description);
URN postURN = postConnection.createPost(post);
```

Retrieve an organization from LinkedIn:

```
VersionedOrganizationConnection connection =
    new VersionedOrganizationConnection(linkedInClient);
Organization organization = connection.retrieveOrganization(organizationU
RN, Parameter
        .with("projection",
            "(elements*(*,roleAssignee~(localizedFirstName,
            localizedLastName),"
                + "organizationalTarget~(localizedName)))"));
```

Discord

There are at least three major Java frameworks for Discord, all very actively developed by the community:

- Discord4J

- Java Discord API (JDA)

- Javacord

Authentication

First, you need to create an application from the Discord Application Dashboard: https://discord.com/developers/applications.

1. Sign in if you're not logged in yet.

2. Click **New Application**.

3. Pick a name, for example, "ApressBookDemoApp", accept the developer terms, and click **Create**.

4. Under **General Information**, you may enter values for the following parameters:

   - Name – This is the name of your application you entered before.

   - App icon – The logo is displayed to users when they authorize with your app.

   - Description – Enter a short description of the application.

   - Tags – Up to five tags to describe the content and functionality of your application.

   - Application ID – The application ID to copy into your application.

   - Public key – The public key to copy into your application.

   - Server count – This is an approximation of the number of servers your application is in. The value is **read only**.

   - Interactions endpoint URL – You can optionally configure an interactions endpoint to receive interactions via HTTP POSTs rather than over Gateway with a bot user.

- Linked roles verification URL – You can configure a verification URL to enable your application as a requirement in a server role's Links settings.

- Terms of Service URL – Link to your application's Terms of Service (optional).

- Privacy policy URL –Link to your privacy policy (optional).

5. Under **OAuth2**, you find the following parameters:

- Client ID – The client ID to copy into your application.

- Client Secret – The client secret to copy into your application. You must regenerate it at first use and be sure to **copy it** as it will not be shown to you again.

- Redirects – You must specify at least one URI for authentication to work. If you pass a URI in an OAuth request, it must exactly match one of the URIs you enter here.

6. Under **Bot**, you find the following parameters:

- Username – This is the name of your bot.

- Icon – The logo is displayed to users of your bot.

- Token – The token to copy into your application. For security purposes, tokens can only be viewed once, when created. If you forgot or lost access to your token, please regenerate a new one.

Discord4J

Discord4J is a reactive Java wrapper for the official Discord API, using reactive principles and the Reactor framework for asynchronous and nonblocking API calls.

Installation

Add the following dependency to the Maven POM of your project:

```
<dependencies>
  <dependency>
    <groupId>com.discord4j</groupId>
```

```
    <artifactId>discord4j-core</artifactId>
    <version>3.2.6</version>
  </dependency>
</dependencies>
```

Quick Example

In the following example, whenever a user sends a !ping message, the bot will
immediately respond with Pong!:

```
public class ExampleBot {
  public static void main(String[] args) {
    String token = args[0];
    DiscordClient client = DiscordClient.create(token);
    GatewayDiscordClient gateway = client.login().block();
    gateway.on(MessageCreateEvent.class).subscribe(event -> {
      Message message = event.getMessage();
      if ("!ping".equals(message.getContent())) {
        MessageChannel channel = message.getChannel().block();
        channel.createMessage("Pong!").block();
      }
    });
    gateway.onDisconnect().block();
  }
}
```

Reactive Example

This example shows the same bot, but in a reactive manner, using Project Reactor:

```
public class ExampleBot {
  public static void main(String[] args) {
    String token = args[0];
    DiscordClient client = DiscordClient.create(token);
    client.login().flatMapMany(gateway -> gateway.
    on(MessageCreateEvent.class))
      .map(MessageCreateEvent::getMessage)
      .filter(message -> "!ping".equals(message.getContent()))
```

```
        .flatMap(Message::getChannel)
        .flatMap(channel -> channel.createMessage("Pong!"))
        .blockLast();
   }
}
```

Sharding Example

This example shows multiple shard groups under the same JVM:

```
// the first group will get even shard IDs
ShardingStrategy first = ShardingStrategy.builder()
        .count(10)
        .filter(s -> s.getIndex() % 2 == 0)
        .build();
// the second group will get odd shard IDs
ShardingStrategy second = ShardingStrategy.builder()
        .count(10)
        .filter(s -> s.getIndex() % 2 != 0)
        .build();
DiscordClient sharedClient = DiscordClient.create(System.getenv("token"));

ShardCoordinator coordinator = LocalShardCoordinator.create();
GatewayDiscordClient firstGroup = sharedClient.gateway()
        .setSharding (first)
        .setEnabledIntents(...)
        .setShardCoordinator(coordinator)
        .login()
        .block();
GatewayDiscordClient secondGroup = sharedClient.gateway()
        .setSharding(second)
        .setEnabledIntents(...)
        .setShardCoordinator(coordinator)
        .login()
        .block();
```

Java Discord API

Java Discord API (JDA, not to be confused with JTA or Jakarta Transactions) aims to offer a clean Java object model around the Discord REST API and Websocket events.

Installation

Add the following dependency to the Maven POM of your project:

```
<dependency>
    <groupId>net.dv8tion</groupId>
    <artifactId>JDA</artifactId>
    <version>VERSION</version>
</dependency>
```

Configuration

Both JDABuilder and DefaultShardManagerBuilder offer a set of configurations:

```
public static void main(String[] args) {
    JDABuilder builder = JDABuilder.createDefault("token");

    // Disable parts of the cache
    builder.disableCache(CacheFlag.MEMBER_OVERRIDES, CacheFlag.
    VOICE_STATE);
    // Enable the bulk delete event
    builder.setBulkDeleteSplittingEnabled(false);
    // Set activity (like "playing Something")
    builder.setActivity(Activity.watching("TV"));

    JDA jda = builder.build();
}
```

EventListener Example

The following example shows how to use the JDA event system:

```
public class ReadyListener implements EventListener
{
    public static void main(String[] args)
```

```
        throws InterruptedException
{
    // Note: It is important to register your ReadyListener before
    building
    JDA jda = JDABuilder.createDefault("token")
        .addEventListeners(new ReadyListener())
        .build();
    // optionally block until JDA is ready
    jda.awaitReady();
}
@Override
public void onEvent(GenericEvent event)
{
    if (event instanceof ReadyEvent)
        System.out.println("API is ready!");
}
}
```

Sharding Example

Discord allows Bot accounts to share load across sessions by limiting them to a fraction of the total connected Guilds/Servers. This can be done using sharding:

```
public static void main(String[] args) throws Exception
{
    JDABuilder shardBuilder = JDABuilder.createDefault("token");
    //register your listeners here using shardBuilder.
    addEventListeners(...)
    shardBuilder.addEventListeners(new MessageListener());
    for (int i = 0; i < 10; i++)
    {
        shardBuilder.useSharding(i, 10)
                    .build();
    }
}
```

Javacord

Javacord is a modern Java library for Discord focusing on simplicity and speed. By reducing itself to standard Java classes and features like `Optional` or `CompletableFuture`, it is easy to learn and use for every Java developer and does not introduce too many concepts or abstractions of its own.

Installation

Add the following dependency to the Maven POM of your project:

```
<dependency>
    <groupId>org.javacord</groupId>
    <artifactId>javacord</artifactId>
    <version>3.8.0</version>
    <type>pom</type>
</dependency>
```

Basic Example

The following example logs the bot in and replies to every "!ping" message with "Pong!". Note that message content is a privileged Intent and needs to be enabled:

```java
public class MyFirstBot {
    public static void main(String[] args) {
        // Insert your bot's token here
        String token = "your token";
        DiscordApi api = new DiscordApiBuilder().setToken(token).
        addIntent(Intent.MESSAGE_CONTENT).login().join();
        // Add a listener which answers with "Pong!" if someone
        writes "!ping"
        api.addMessageCreateListener(event -> {
            if (event.getMessageContent().equalsIgnoreCase("!ping")) {
                event.getChannel().sendMessage("Pong!");
            }
        });
        // Print the invite url of your bot
```

```
        System.out.println("You can invite the bot by using the following
        url: " + api.createBotInvite());
    }
}
```

Slash Command Example

The following example shows how we can let the bot send answers to a simple slash command:

```java
public class MyFirstBot {
    public static void main(String[] args) {
        String token = "your token";
        DiscordApi api = new DiscordApiBuilder().setToken(token).
        login().join();
        api.addSlashCommandCreateListener(event -> {
            SlashCommandInteraction slashCommandInteraction = event.
            getSlashCommandInteraction();
            if (slashCommandInteraction.getCommandName().equals("ping")) {
                slashCommandInteraction.createImmediateResponder()
                    .setContent("Pong!")
                    .setFlags(MessageFlag.EPHEMERAL) // Only visible for
                    the user which invoked the command
                    .respond();
            }
        });
    }
}
```

MessageBuilder Example

The following example uses the built-in `MessageBuilder`. It is very useful to construct complex messages with images, code blocks, embeds, or attachments:

```java
public class MyListener implements MessageCreateListener {
    @Override
    public void onMessageCreate(MessageCreateEvent event) {
```

```
        Message message = event.getMessage();
        if (message.getContent().equalsIgnoreCase("!ping")) {
            event.getChannel().sendMessage("Pong!");
        }
    }
}
```

EventListener Example

For better readability, it is also possible to have listeners in their own class:

```
public class MyListener implements MessageCreateListener {
    @Override
    public void onMessageCreate(MessageCreateEvent event) {
        Message message = event.getMessage();
        if (message.getContent().equalsIgnoreCase("!ping")) {
            event.getChannel().sendMessage("Pong!");
        }
    }
}
```

Calling the listener:

```
api.addListener(new MyListener());
```

Twitch4J

Twitch4J is a Java and JVM-based API client for the Twitch REST API Interfaces. It supports Java, Kotlin, and Groovy.

Installation

Add the following dependency to your Maven project POM:

```
<dependency>
    <groupId>com.github.twitch4j</groupId>
    <artifactId>twitch4j</artifactId>
    <version>1.16.0</version>
</dependency>
```

Usage and Examples

Get an access token:

1. Log in to the developer console `https://dev.twitch.tv/console` using your Twitch account. If you don't have an account, select the **Sign Up** tab to create one.

   - When you sign up for an account, Twitch sends you an email to verify your account. Be sure to open the email and verify your account before proceeding.

   - You must also enable two-factor authentication (2FA) for your account. To enable 2FA, navigate to Security and Privacy, and follow the steps for enabling 2FA under the Security section.

   - You'll need to refresh your console for these changes to take effect.

2. Select the **Applications** tab on the developer console and then click **Register Your Application**.

3. Set **Name** to your application's name. The name must be unique among all Twitch applications. Your app's name is listed on the Connections page under **Other Connections** if your app requires user consent to access or modify the user's resources.

4. Set **OAuth Redirect URLs** to the callback URL that your app uses for authorizations. After adding your redirect URL, click **Add**.

5. Select a **Category** (type of application) that your app belongs to.

6. Click the **I'm not a robot** check box.

7. Click **Create**.

8. Back in the **Applications** tab, locate your app under **Developer Applications**, and click **Manage**.

9. Note your **Client ID**, which you'll use to get your access token and to set the Client-Id header in all API requests. Client IDs are considered public and can be embedded in a web page's source.

10. Depending on the flow you use to get a token, you may need a client secret. For example, the Authorization Code Grant Flow requires a client secret. Click **New Secret** to generate a secret that you'll use to get your access token. You must copy the secret and store it somewhere safe. Getting a new secret invalidates the previous secret, which might make your API requests fail until you update your app.

Initialize and configure Twitch4J Client:

```
TwitchClient twitchClient = TwitchClientBuilder.builder()
.withEnableHelix(true)
.build();
```

Channels

Join a channel

```
twitchClient.getChat().joinChannel("PlayOverwatch");
```

Write Channel Chat to the Console

```
public class WriteChannelChatToConsole {
    /**
     * Register events of this class with the EventManager/EventHandler
     *
     * @param eventHandler SimpleEventHandler
     */
    public WriteChannelChatToConsole(SimpleEventHandler eventHandler) {
        eventHandler.onEvent(ChannelMessageEvent.class, event ->
        onChannelMessage(event));
    }
    /**
     * Subscribe to the ChannelMessage Event and write the output to
       the console
     */
    public void onChannelMessage(ChannelMessageEvent event) {
        System.out.printf(
                "Channel [%s] - User[%s] - Message [%s]%n",
```

```
            event.getChannel().getName(),
            event.getUser().getName(),
            event.getMessage()
        );
    }
}
```

Clips

Create a clip

```
CreateClipList clipData = twitchClient.getHelix().createClip(accessToken,
"149223493", false).execute();
clipData.getData().forEach(clip -> {
System.out.println("Created Clip with ID: " + clip.getId());
});
```

Write a clip's ID to the Console

```
ClipList clipList = twitchClient.getHelix().getClips(null, "488552", null,
null, null, null, null, null).execute();
clipList.getData().forEach(clip -> {
System.out.println("Found Clip: " + clip.getId());
});
```

Games

Write a game's ID and name to the Console

```
GameList resultList = twitchClient.getHelix().getGames(Arrays.
asList(overwatchGameId), null).execute();
resultList.getGames().forEach(game -> {
System.out.println("Game ID: " + game.getId() + " is " + game.getName());
});
```

Vertical Frameworks

Vertical Social Frameworks allow the integration with domain-specific social networks.

GitHub

While GitHub/Microsoft itself has no official Java API for GitHub, there are two actively maintained APIs offering a domain model, besides several others that support it on an REST/OpenID Connect level:

- GitHub API for Java

- GitHub Java Client

Both offer a variety of authentication methods, including a personal access token.

Token Generation

To generate a new token for GitHub REST APIs:

1. Log in to the GitHub Account

2. Go to Settings ➤ Developer settings ➤ Personal access tokens

3. Click on generate a new token

4. Confirm the user password to continue

5. Add a description to the token

6. Under the select scopes option, check all the boxes

7. Click on generate a new token

GitHub API for Java

GitHub API for Java provides an object model around the GitHub REST API. Its creation is led by Kohsuke Kawaguchi, the "father" of Jenkins CI.

Authentication

The GitHub Java library offers multiple authentication methods:

- Username and password (not recommended, except for development purposes)

- Personal access token

- JWT token

- GitHub app installation token

  - User

  - Organization

Usage Examples

We use a personal access token, following the steps for Token Generation.

Repositories

Here's an example of using the GitHub API for Java to connect against GitHub and create a new repository before cleaning it up again:

```
GitHub github = new GitHubBuilder().withOAuthToken("my_personal_token").
build();

GHRepository repo = github.createRepository(
  "new-repository","this is my new repository",
  "https://www.kohsuke.org/",true/*public*/);
repo.addCollaborators(github.getUser("abcde"),github.getUser("jdoe"));
repo.delete();
```

Organizations

To create resources in GitHub for an organization, you must create an object of type GHOrganization:

```
GHOrganization organizationClient(GitHub github, String organizationName)
throws IOException {
        return github.getOrganization(organizationName);
    }
```

Now we can work with the GHOrganization. Creating a repository or any other methods to create resources will do so under that organization:

```
void createRepository(GHOrganization organization) {
  organization.createRepository("repository-name")
            .private_(true)
```

```
                  .wiki(false)
                  .projects(false)
                  .description("Description")
                  .allowMergeCommit(true)
                  .allowSquashMerge(false)
                  .allowRebaseMerge(false)
                  .create()
    }
```

GitHub Java Client

GitHub Java Client is a small Java library for talking to GitHub/GitHub Enterprise and interacting with projects. It is maintained by the Swedish Social Music Streaming portal Spotify. It supports authentication via access tokens, JWT endpoints, and GitHub Apps (via private key).

Installation

Include the latest version of github-client into your project POM:

```
<dependency>
  <groupId>com.spotify</groupId>
  <artifactId>github-client</artifactId>
  <version>version</version>
</dependency>
```

Usage Examples

We use a personal access token, following the steps for Token Generation:

```
final GitHubClient githubClient = GitHubClient.create(URI.create("https://
api.github.com/"), "my-access-token");
```

This client attempts to mirror the GitHub API endpoints. As an example, to get details of a commit, use the GET /repos/:owner/:repo/commits API call, under the repos API. Therefore, getCommit lives under the RepositoryClient:

```
final RepositoryClient repositoryClient = githubClient.
createRepositoryClient("my-org", "my-repo");
log.info(repositoryClient.getCommit("sha").get().htmlUrl());
```

Repositories

Methods related to check runs or issues are also located under the RepositoryClient:

```
final ChecksClient checksClient = repositoryClient.createChecksApiClient();
checksClient.createCheckRun(CHECK_RUN_REQUEST);
final IssueClient issueClient = repositoryClient.createIssueClient();
issueClient.createComment(ISSUE_ID, "comment body")
  .thenAccept(comment -> log.info("created comment " + comment.htmlUrl()));
```

Organizations

Methods related to teams and memberships are located under the OrganisationClient:

```
final TeamClient teamClient = organisationClient.createTeamClient();
final Membership membership =  teamClient.getMembership("teamname");
```

Uber

Similar to Meta, Uber maintains its own SDKs for a number of popular languages including Java.

Java SDK

The following examples show how to use the Java Rides SDK.

First, you need to register your app on the Uber Developer Dashboard: https://developer.uber.com/dashboard/.

Installation

Add the following dependencies to your project (Gradle because it supports both Java and Kotlin/Android):

```
dependencies {
    compile 'com.uber.sdk:rides:0.5.2'
}
```

Use the latest version where available.

Examples

Get an Uber session with a server token

When you registered your app, you were given a server token, client ID, and client secret. Use them to authenticate your application:

```
SessionConfiguration config = new SessionConfiguration.Builder()
    .setClientId("<CLIENT_ID>")
    .setServerToken("<SERVER_TOKEN>")
    .build();
ServerTokenSession session = new ServerTokenSession(config);
```

Get a list of available products

```
Response<List<Product>> response = service.getProducts(37.79f, -122.39f).
execute();
List<Product> products = response.body();
String productId = products.get(0).getProductId();
```

Get estimates for time and price

```
Response<TimeEstimatesResponse> response = service.
getPickupTimeEstimate(37.79f, -122.39f, productId).execute()
```

Request a ride

```
# Get products for location
Response<List<Product>> response = service.getProducts(37.79f, -122.39f).
execute();
List<Product> products = response.body();
String productId = products.get(0).getProductId();
# Get upfront fare for product with start/end location
RideRequestParameters rideRequestParameters = new RideRequestParameters.
Builder().setPickupCoordinates(37.77f, -122.41f)
        .setProductId(productId)
        .setDropoffCoordinates(37.49f, -122.41f)
```

```
        .build();
RideEstimate rideEstimate = service.estimateRide(rideRequestParameters).
execute().body();
String fareId = rideEstimate.getFareId();
# Request ride with upfront fare for product with start/end location
RideRequestParameters rideRequestParameters = new RideRequestParameters.
Builder().setPickupCoordinates(37.77f, -122.41f)
        .setProductId(productId)
        .setFareId(fareId)
        .setDropoffCoordinates(37.49f, -122.41f)
        .build();
Ride ride = service.requestRide(rideRequestParameters).execute().body();
String rideId = ride.getRideId();
# Request ride details from request_id
Ride ride = service.getRideDetails(rideId).execute().body();
# Cancel a ride
Response<Void> response = service.cancelRide(rideId).execute();
```

Legacy Frameworks

Although many are still in productive use, the following social frameworks are no longer actively maintained or supported by the contributors.

Agorava

Agorava [33] is a social framework providing CDI modules, contexts, and extensions to interact with major social networks or similar services exposing APIs. It offers these services to Java and Java Enterprise applications and eases mixing them in the spirit of mashups. [12]

History

You'll remember the origin and predecessors to Agorava from Chapter 3 where we discussed standardization efforts and JSR 357 turned down by a majority of JCP EC members, resulting in Agorava being created as a successor to Seam Social. With co-founder Antoine Sabot-Durand contributing to JBoss projects like CDI, which he became Spec Lead after joining JBoss in 2013, it was also featured in the JBoss stack for some time [56], although not an official part of projects like WildFly, etc. Agorava was mentioned in the JBoss developer framework (JDF) for social applications, but when JDF was rebranded to "Quickstarts," most of these tutorials were abandoned or archived.

Therefore, similar to Spring Social mostly superseded by Spring Security, the same happened with Agorava and Jakarta Security, especially from Jakarta EE 10 onward, or Keycloak replacing PicketLink in the JBoss/Red Hat stack.

Overview

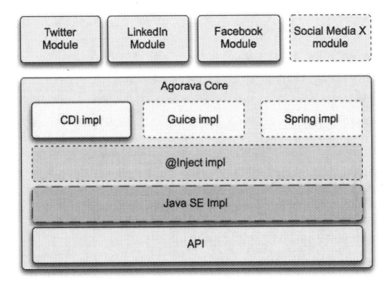

Figure 6-1. *Agorava Macro Architecture*

These are the main features of Agorava:

- Confidentiality

- A generic portable REST client API

- A generic API to handle OAuth 1.0a and 2.0 services

- A generic API to work with JSON serialization and deserialization

- A generic identification API to retrieve basic user information from a social service (as identity provider)

- A multiservice manager API allowing to deal with multiple OAuth applications and sessions in the same application

- Out of the box, Agorava connects to

- Facebook

- LinkedIn

- GitHub

- Twitter

- XING

- And offers an easy way to extend it by creating new connectors to any other service or API

Agorava is independent of CDI implementation and fully portable between Java EE 6 (minimum) and Servlet environments enhanced by CDI. It can be also used with CDI in Java SE in a Desktop or SE Embedded/Mobile application. It has been fully tested with the CDI RI implementation (JBoss Weld). OpenWebBeans and Caucho Resin were also supported since the 0.5 release.

Agorava is often explained as a sort of "Java Connector Architecture for Social." And indeed, there are striking similarities between the idea behind Agorava and what Jakarta Connectors (formerly JCA) does under the Jakarta EE umbrella.

Jakarta Connectors defines a standard architecture for connecting the Jakarta EE platform to heterogeneous Enterprise Information Systems (EIS) including transaction processing systems such as CICS Transaction Server and Enterprise Resource Planning (ERP) systems like SAP, especially the so-called Common Client Interface (CCI), which defined a standard client API allowing applications to access multiple resource adapters.

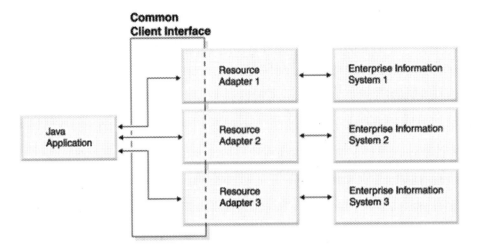

Figure 6-2. JCA Common Client Interface

One must add JCA is a fairly old part of the Jakarta EE platform, which received a few minor changes when JCA became Jakarta Connectors, but otherwise it is still quite old, similar to, for example, Jakarta Enterprise Beans (EJB). So compared to some of the new, often cloud native and API-based ERP solutions along the lines of Salesforce.com, it seems a bit outdated and is also among the lesser known and used parts of Jakarta EE.

Though the JSR 357 proposal did not explicitly phrase it the "JCA way," it is also possible some of the supporters and JCA experts (besides Oracle that was mostly IBM or SAP, most other companies now dominating in the Cloud didn't even exist when JCA was originally designed) felt the little "dinosaur" they fostered could be threatened by a new standard like a Java Social Connector API.

Core

Agorava Core includes common, social networking services that are independent of a particular service provider, offering features such as

- OAuth connectors to authenticate against OAuth providers

- Support for generic authentication and user profile management

- A social multi-account service supporting

- Multiple social network connections

- Multiple sessions for the same social network provider, for example, connected to multiple user accounts or queries at the same time

Agorava Core also provides implementations of these services. The main implementation is based on CDI and DeltaSpike right now, but most services have been generalized using JSR 330 (now Jakarta Dependency Injection), which allows more lightweight Java SE alternatives like Google Guice, Dagger, or the SE version of the CDI Implementation Weld.

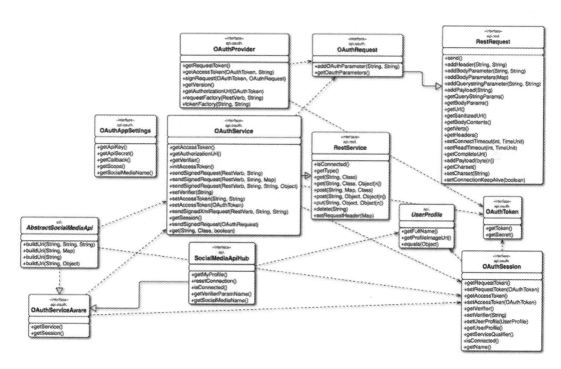

Figure 6-3. *Agorava Core API Architecture*

Agorava PicketLink

Working together with OAuth functionality and user profile management, Agorava Core also contains a security subsystem based on PicketLink.

As promised in 2.3.2, here is the specialized Agorava version of the PicketLink BaseAuthenticator:

```
@Generic
public class AgoravaAuthenticator extends BaseAuthenticator {
    @InjectWithQualifier
    OAuthAppSettings settings;
    @Inject
```

```
DefaultLoginCredentials credentials;

@Inject
@DeltaSpike
Instance<HttpServletResponse> response;
@Inject
OAuthLifeCycleService lifeCycleService;

@Override
public void authenticate() {
    if (lifeCycleService.getCurrentSession().isConnected()) {
        OAuthSession session = lifeCycleService.getCurrentSession();
        UserProfile userProfile = session.getUserProfile();
        credentials.setCredential(session.getAccessToken());
        setStatus(AuthenticationStatus.SUCCESS);

        User user = new User(userProfile.getId());
        user.setFirstName(userProfile.getFullName());
        setAccount(user);
    } else {
        String authorizationUrl = lifeCycleService.
        startDanceFor(settings.getQualifier());
        try {
            response.get().sendRedirect(authorizationUrl);
        } catch (IOException e) {
            e.printStackTrace();
        }
        credentials.setStatus(Status.IN_PROGRESS);
        setStatus(AuthenticationStatus.DEFERRED);
    }
}
}
```

Connectors

Agorava currently comes with default connectors to

- Facebook

- LinkedIn

- GitHub

- Twitter

- XING

In addition to those, third-party Agorava Connectors were created for services like

- Empire Avenue

- Google+

- Instagram

- Meetup

- Stack Overflow

- TripIt

- WordPress

- Yammer

Socializer

Socializer is a real-life demonstration web app for Agorava; think of it as its "Pet Clinic."

It allows you to connect to various social networks and see your timeline or post updates. Agorava Socializer was also ported from JavaServer Faces to the Apache Wicket Web Framework or AngularJS.

Both ports were still rather experimental and therefore never became official parts of the Agorava ecosystem.

Integrating a Connector

Adding a new connector to Socializer is quite easy. We'll take the XING connector as an example of how to do it.

After cloning `https://github.com/agorava/agorava-socializer` the following lines in the Socializer **pom.xml**

```
<!-- xing -->
    <dependency>
            <groupId>org.agorava</groupId>
                        <artifactId>agorava-xing-api</artifactId>
            <version>0.3.0-SNAPSHOT</version>
            <scope>compile</scope>
    </dependency>
    <dependency>
            <groupId>org.agorava</groupId>
            <artifactId>agorava-xing-cdi</artifactId>
            <version>0.3.0-SNAPSHOT</version>
            <scope>runtime</scope>
    </dependency>
```

define dependencies for XING API and CDI Implementation.

Next, we add the app settings for XING to CDI producer class `org.agorava.socializer.SettingsProducer.java`:

```
@ApplicationScoped
@Produces
@Xing
@OAuthApplication(params = {@Param(name = OAuthAppSettingsBuilder.PREFIX,
value = "xing")})
    public OAuthAppSettings xingSettings;
```

Backed by the properties file

```
src/main/resources/local/agorava.properties
xing.apiKey=<your API Key>
xing.apiSecret=<your API Secret>
```

Both **API key** and **API secret** have to be defined for a local Socializer application in the social media account of your choice; see `https://dev.xing.com/applications/` dashboard for XING.

xing.xhtml

```
<ui:composition xmlns="http://www.w3.org/1999/xhtml"
            xmlns:ui="http://java.sun.com/jsf/facelets"
            xmlns:f="http://java.sun.com/jsf/core"
            xmlns:h="http://java.sun.com/jsf/html"
            xmlns:p="http://primefaces.org/ui">

        <h:panelGroup id="xingtl" layout="block">
            <div class="well">
                <h6>What's on your mind?</h6>
                <p>
                        <p:inputTextarea value="#{socialClient.
                        status}" styleClass="post-area" />
                </p>
            </div>
        </h:panelGroup>
</ui:composition>
```

Most proper services offer a "Test key" or development key like XING does.

To get Facebook App Id and App secret credentials, you will need to create a new application with Facebook at `https://developers.facebook.com/apps/`.

Spring Social

The Spring Social project [25] is an extension of the Spring Framework that enables your applications to establish connections with social media providers like Facebook, LinkedIn, or Twitter to invoke APIs on behalf of their users.

After some time, it was not actively supported, and updates or blog posts by Pivotal/ VMware staff appeared six to nine months or longer after a change was made or a feature announced at a conference.

Open source ecosystems like GitHub show various extensions or plug-ins, but not all of them were mature; some were merely a PoC, and most of them have not been actively maintained for some time either.

Spring Social also supported .NET, but that never even took off and only two versions, 1.0.0 followed by 1.0.1, were released in 2012, without any further activity after that. So while the Spring Framework for .NET still exists and is maintained, with version 3.0.2 released in July 2023, Spring Social for .NET died many years before its Java counterpart.

Due to increased standardization of OAuth2/OpenID Connect and its support in Spring Security 5, Spring Social is no longer supported or maintained since 2019. The support period ended on July 3, 2019. Which does not mean applications completely abandoned it, even in production, but for new ones, they would usually prefer Spring Security, while for some old ones that are no longer changed but still used, they may use it, as long as the API changes by social networks do not prevent it after some time.

Overview

The main features of Spring Social are as follows:

- Extensible service provider framework that greatly simplifies the process of connecting local user accounts to social media accounts

- A connect controller that handles the authorization flow between your Java/Spring web application, a social media provider, and your users

- Java bindings to popular APIs and social networks like Facebook, Twitter, LinkedIn, TripIt, or GitHub

- A sign-in controller that enables users to authenticate with your application by signing in through a social network

The Maven `groupID` of Spring Social is `org.springframework.social`.

Core

The Spring Social core projects consist of modules shown in Table 6-2.

Table 6-2. *Spring Social Core Modules*

Name	Description
spring-social-core	Spring Social connect framework and OAuth client support
spring-social-config	Java and XML configuration support for Spring Social
spring-social-security	Spring Security integration
spring-social-web	Spring Social ConnectController using the connect framework to manage connections in a web environment

Client Modules

In addition to the Spring Social core modules, there are a number of provider-specific client modules providing connectivity and API bindings to popular social networks.

Table 6-3. *Spring Social Client Modules*

Name	Maven artifactID
Spring Social Facebook	spring-social-facebook
Spring Social Twitter	spring-social-twitter
Spring Social LinkedIn	spring-social-linkedin
Spring Social GitHub	spring-social-github
Spring Social TripIt	spring-social-tripit

Connect Framework

The Connection<A> interface models a connection to a service provider like Facebook:

```java
public interface Connection<A> extends Serializable {

    ConnectionKey getKey();

    String getDisplayName();

    String getProfileUrl();

    String getImageUrl();

    void sync();

    boolean test();

    boolean hasExpired();

    void refresh();

    UserProfile fetchUserProfile();

    void updateStatus(String message);

    A getApi();

    ConnectionData createData();

}
```

Each Connection is uniquely identified by a composite key consisting of providerId (e.g., "facebook") and providerUserId (e.g., the user's Facebook ID).

Let's assume we have a Connection<Twitter> reference to a user "jdoe".

1. Connection#getKey() returns "twitter", 1234567, where 1234567 is @jdoe's Twitter user id that never changes.

2. Connection#getDisplayName() returns @jdoe.

3. Connection#getProfileUrl() returns "http://twitter.com/jdoe".

4. Connection#getImageUrl() returns *"http://a0.twimg.com/profile_images/105951287/IMG_5863_2_normal.jpg"*.

5. `Connection#sync()` allows you to synchronize the state of the connection with @jdoe's profile.

6. `Connection#test()` returns `true` indicating the authorization credentials of the Twitter connection are valid. This assumes Twitter has not revoked the "AcmeApp" client application, and @jdoe has not reset his authorization credentials.

7. `Connection#hasExpired()` returns `false`.

8. `Connection#refresh()` does nothing, as long as connections to Twitter don't expire.

9. `Connection#fetchUserProfile()` makes a remote call to the Twitter API to get @jdoe's profile data and normalize it into a `UserProfile` model.

10. `Connection#updateStatus(String)` posts a status update on @jdoe's timeline.

11. `Connection#getApi()` returns a reference giving the client application access to the full capabilities of Twitter's native API.

12. `Connection#createData()` returns a `ConnectionData` reference that could be serialized and used to restore the connection at a later point.

Facebook Example

This example shows how to add a Facebook login to an existing Spring web app using Spring Social.

To get Facebook App Id and App secret credentials, you will need to create a new application with Facebook at `https://developers.facebook.com/apps/`.

Make sure to add "Website" as platform and `http://localhost:8080/` as the "Site URL".

Maven Config

First, add the spring-social-facebook dependency to the pom.xml:

```
<dependency>
    <groupId>org.springframework.social</groupId>
    <artifactId>spring-social-facebook</artifactId>
    <version>2.0.3.RELEASE</version>
</dependency>
```

Security Config

Let's use a simple security configuration with form-based authentication:

```java
@Configuration
@EnableWebSecurity
@ComponentScan(basePackages = { "com.example.security" })
public class SecurityConfig {

    @Autowired
    private UserDetailsService userDetailsService;

    @Bean
    public AuthenticationManager authManager(HttpSecurity http) throws
    Exception {
        return http.getSharedObject(AuthenticationManagerBuilder.class)
            .userDetailsService(userDetailsService)
            .and()
            .build();
    }

    @Bean
    public SecurityFilterChain filterChain(HttpSecurity http) throws
    Exception {
        http.csrf()
            .disable()
            .authorizeRequests()
            .antMatchers("/login*", "/signin/**", "/signup/**")
            .permitAll()
            .anyRequest()
```

```
            .authenticated()
            .and()
            .formLogin()
            .loginPage("/login")
            .permitAll()
            .and()
            .logout();
        return http.build();
    }
}
```

Facebook4J

Facebook4J is an unofficial Java library for the Facebook Graph API. It was modelled after Twitter4J, hence the similar name.

Using It

Include the following dependency in your Maven **pom.xml**:

```
<dependency>
  <groupId>org.facebook4j</groupId>
  <artifactId>facebook4j-core</artifactId>
  <version>[2.4,)</version>
</dependency>
```

Configuration

There are several ways to configure Facebook4J.

Properties file

A properties file named facebook4j.properties. Place it to either the root of the Classpath:

```
debug=true
oauth.appId=***************
oauth.appSecret=*****************************
oauth.accessToken=****************************
oauth.permissions=email,publish_stream,...
```

ConfigurationBuilder

You could use a "Fluent" API via ConfigurationBuilder and FacebookFactory:

```
ConfigurationBuilder cb = new ConfigurationBuilder();
cb.setDebugEnabled(true)
  .setOAuthAppId("********************")
  .setOAuthAppSecret("****************************************")
  .setOAuthAccessToken("****************************************
  *******")
  .setOAuthPermissions("email,publish_stream,...");
FacebookFactory ff = new FacebookFactory(cb.build());
Facebook facebook = ff.getInstance();
```

Or via System Properties

```
$ java -Dfacebook4j.debug=true
    -Dfacebook4j.oauth.appId=********************
    -Dfacebook4j.oauth.appSecret=**********************************************
    -Dfacebook4j.oauth.
     accessToken=************************************************
    -Dfacebook4j.oauth.permissions=email,publish_stream,...
    -cp facebook4j-core-2.4.13.jar:yourApp.jar yourpackage.Main
```

As well as environment variables (example for Linux)

```
$ export facebook4j.debug=true
$ export facebook4j.oauth.appId=********************
$ export facebook4j.oauth.
appSecret=****************************************
$ export facebook4j.oauth.
accessToken=************************************************
$ export facebook4j.oauth.permissions=email,publish_stream,...
$ java -cp facebook4j-core-2.4.13.jar:yourApp.jar yourpackage.Main
```

While the Fluent API may seem attractive in modern applications, the other options can be easier to externalize the secrets via Kubernetes or the CI/CD pipeline of your choice.

Examples

Publishing a Message

You can publish a message via the Facebook.postStatusMessage() method, assuming you configured Facebook4J via one of the methods mentioned before:

```
Facebook facebook = new FacebookFactory().getInstance();
facebook.postStatusMessage("Hello World from Facebook4J.");
```

Search for Places

```
Facebook facebook = new FacebookFactory().getInstance();
// Search by name
ResponseList<Place> results = facebook.searchPlaces("coffee");

// You can narrow your search to a specific location and distance
GeoLocation center = new GeoLocation(37.76, -122.427);
int distance = 1000;
ResponseList<Place> searchPlaces("coffee", center, distance);
```

Execute FQL

You can execute FQL via the Facebook.executeFQL() method:

```
Facebook facebook = new FacebookFactory().getInstance();

// Single FQL
String query = "SELECT uid2 FROM friend WHERE uid1=me()";
JSONArray jsonArray = facebook.executeFQL(query);
for (int i = 0; i < jsonArray.length(); i++) {
    JSONObject jsonObject = jsonArray.getJSONObject(i);
    System.out.println(jsonObject.get("uid2"));
}

// Multiple FQL
Map<String, String> queries = new HashMap<>();
queries.put("all friends", "SELECT uid2 FROM friend WHERE uid1=me()");
queries.put("my name", "SELECT name FROM user WHERE uid=me()");
Map<String, JSONArray> result = facebook.executeMultiFQL(queries);
JSONArray allFriendsJSONArray = result.get("all friends");
for (int i = 0; i < allFriendsJSONArray.length(); i++) {
```

```
    JSONObject jsonObject = allFriendsJSONArray.getJSONObject(i);
    System.out.println(jsonObject.get("uid2"));
}
JSONArray myNameJSONArray = result.get("my name");
System.out.println(myNameJSONArray.getJSONObject(0).get("name"));
```

Batch Mode

Similar to the Meta Business SDK, you can execute Batch Requests via the Facebook.
executeBatch() method:

```
Facebook facebook = new FacebookFactory().getInstance();

// Executing "me" and "me/friends?limit=50" endpoints
BatchRequests<BatchRequest> batch = new BatchRequests<BatchRequest>();
batch.add(new BatchRequest(RequestMethod.GET, "me"));
batch.add(new BatchRequest(RequestMethod.GET, "me/friends?limit=50"));
List<BatchResponse> results = facebook.executeBatch(batch);

BatchResponse result1 = results.get(0);
BatchResponse result2 = results.get(1);

// You can get http status code or headers
int statusCode1 = result1.getStatusCode();
String contentType = result1.getResponseHeader("Content-Type");

// You can get body content via as****() method
String jsonString = result1.asString();
JSONObject jsonObject = result1.asJSONObject();
ResponseList<JSONObject> responseList = result2.asResponseList ();

// You can map json to java object using DataObjectFactory#create****()
User user = DataObjectFactory.createUser(jsonString);
Friend friend1 = DataObjectFactory.createFriend(responseList.get(0).
toString());
Friend friend2 = DataObjectFactory.createFriend(responseList.get(1).
toString());
```

Summary

Following an overview of security frameworks in the previous chapter, we learned about relevant social frameworks for the Java platform and how to use them with popular social networks in this chapter.

CHAPTER 7

Social Portals

As you remember from Chapter 3, Java Portlets were an early approach to mashups; therefore, popular portal servers also support social media integration like social login, mashups, or social sharing.

Liferay Portal

Liferay is a "professional open source" company providing paid support and services for its open source portal software.

History

Liferay Portal was initially created in 2000 by co-founder and CTO Brian Chan to provide a portal solution to NGOs like churches. The first office of Liferay was also in a church.

Liferay Inc. forged partnerships with Sun, shortly before it was acquired by Oracle, or TIBCO, but it remained independent and privately owned until now. With open source in its DNA, Liferay also actively helped shape the Java Portlet standards like JSR 362 (Portlet 3.0) or 378 (Portlet 3.0 Bridge for JavaServer Faces 2.2), in this case as the Spec Lead.

Liferay Social

Whether you want to create your own social media experience or integrate other social networks, you can do both with Liferay Portal.

© Werner Keil 2024
W. Keil, *Enterprise Social for the Java Platform*, https://doi.org/10.1007/978-1-4842-9571-7_7

Out of the box, Liferay offers four social portlets:

- Activities

- User statistics

- Group statistics

- Requests

Besides those, integrations exist for various APIs and social networks.

Map Portlet

The Map portlet allows you to view the locations of team members around the world, but only members of the site to which the Map portlet has been added are displayed.

First, you'll need a key from Google to access Google's Maps API with the Map portlet. Visit `https://developers.google.com/maps/documentation/javascript/tutorial#api_key` to obtain a valid Google Maps API key.

Then perform the following steps:

1. Install the Social Networking plug-in, if you haven't done so already.

2. Install the IP Geocoder portlet. (Both the Social Networking and IP Geocoder apps are available from Liferay Marketplace.)

3. Shut down your portal server.

4. Download the Geo Lite City database from `https://mirrors-cdn.liferay.com/geolite.maxmind.com/download/geoip/database/GeoLiteCityv6.dat.gz`.

5. Unzip the `.dat` file to your desired location.

6. Create a `portlet-ext.properties` file in the `/{ROOT}/webapps/ip-geocoder-portlet/WEB-INF/classes/` directory of your Liferay installation.

7. Add the property `maxmind.database.file={GeoLite City .dat file path}` to this file.

   On Windows, make sure the file path is separated by \\, for example, `C:\\ce\\bundles\\GeoLiteCity.dat`.

8. Create a `portlet-ext.properties` file in the `/{ROOT}/webapps/social-networking-portlet/WEB-INF/classes/` directory of your Liferay installation.

9. Add the property `map.google.maps.api.key={Your API Key}` to this file, using the Google Maps API Key generated earlier.

10. Restart your portal server.

11. Use the Map Portlet.

Social Network Integration

There are several ways to integrate Liferay Portal with social networks like Facebook, LinkedIn, Twitter/X, or others.

Facebook Login

You can set up Facebook as a single sign-on mechanism for Liferay DXP.

Facebook Connect SSO authentication is an integration of Liferay with Facebook's Graph API. To retrieve the user's Facebook profile information and match it to existing Liferay DXP users. When new Liferay DXP users are added this way, they are created by retrieving the following four fields from Facebook:

- Email address
- First name
- Last name
- Gender

To get Facebook App ID and App secret credentials:

1. Go to `https://developers.facebook.com/apps/`.

2. Click ***Create new App***.

3. Enter the values for the following parameters:

   a) Display name – The name of your application that is displayed at the end of each post, for example, your company name.

   b) Namespace – Optional value that is used to access Facebook Insights. It is recommended to use a unique name for each application you set up.

c) Category – A category matching your business type. If unsure, select ***Apps for Pages***.

4. Click ***Create App***.

5. You get to a configuration screen for your application. Select ***Settings*** and enter the following:

   a) App domain – A comma-separated list of domains or IP addresses you want to use for this application with individual Facebook accounts. You are able to authorize your application from one of the domains/addresses in that list.

6. Click ***Add Platform*** and select ***Website***.

7. Set ***Site URL*** and (if applicable) ***Mobile Site URL*** to the desired website, for example, `http://www.mysite.com`.

8. Click ***Save Changes***.

9. Now you see the ***App ID/API Key*** and ***App Secret*** for your application.

To configure the Facebook Connect SSO module at the Liferay system level, navigate to Liferay DXP's Control Panel ➤ Configuration ➤ System Settings, and find the ***Facebook Connect*** module under the Foundation heading. Values configured there provide default values for all portal instances.

To override these defaults for a particular portal instance, navigate to the Liferay DXP Control Panel, click ***Instance Settings***, and find ***Facebook*** within the Authentication section.

- Enabled – Check this to enable Facebook Connect SSO authentication.

- Require Verified Account – Check this to allow logins by Facebook users who have gone through the Facebook email verification process to prove that they can access the email address they provided when they registered.

- Application ID – Can only be set at the portal instance level. Enter the ID of your registered Facebook application.

- Application Secret – Can only be set at the portal instance level. Enter the secret of your registered Facebook application.

- Graph URL – The base URL of Facebook graph API. Only change this if Facebook changes their Graph API. As long as Facebook's API remains the same, use the default graph URL.

- OAuth Authorization URL – Facebook OAuth authorization URL. You will only need to change this if Facebook changes their OAuth authorization endpoint. This URL will be decorated with dynamic data and linked to from the Liferay Sign In portlet.

- OAuth Token URL – Facebook OAuth access token URL. Liferay DXP uses this URL to exchange a request token for an access token.

- OAuth Redirect URL – The URL users will be directed to once an OAuth request token has been generated. The URL points to a Liferay DXP service that exchanges the request token for the access token, required in order for Liferay DXP to successfully call the Facebook Graph API. You should only need to change this URL if requests to Liferay DXP go through a proxy server like Apache doing URL rewriting.

Social Bookmarks

Social bookmarks appear below content as buttons to share it on social networks. For example, social bookmarks appear by default in the Blogs widget below each blog post.

These social bookmarks are available by default:

- Facebook

- LinkedIn

- Twitter/X

In addition, the social bookmarks app on Liferay Marketplace adds further social bookmarks for social networks like

- Digg

- Evernote

- Reddit

- Slashdot

OpenSocial

Like other open standards, Liferay supports the OpenSocial framework and specifications (although pre-W3C with Apache Shindig, as it looks like)

You can publish gadgets found online, or you can use Liferay Portal's OpenSocial gadget editor to create and publish your own gadgets:

Here's an example for a PubSub Publisher gadget:

```xml
<?xml version="1.0"?>
<Module>
    <ModulePrefs height="250" title="Sample PubSub Publisher">
        <Require feature="pubsub-2">
            <Param name="topics">
                <![CDATA[
                    <Topic
        description="Publishes a random number."
            name="org.apache.shindig.random-number"
                        publish="true"
                        title="Random Number"
                        type="number"
                    />
                ]]>
            </Param>
        </Require>
    </ModulePrefs>
    <Content type="html">
        <![CDATA[
            <script>
                function publish() {
                    var message = Math.random();
                gadgets.Hub.publish('org.apache.shindig.random-number',
                message);
                    document.getElementById('output').innerHTML =
                    message;
                }
            </script>
```

```
            <div>
                    <input onclick="publish();" type="button" value=
                    "Publish a Random Number" />
            </div>
            <div id="output">
            </div>
        ]]>
    </Content>
</Module>
```

Here a PubSub Subscriber gadget example:

```
<?xml version="1.0"?>
<Module>
    <ModulePrefs height="250" title="Sample PubSub Subscriber">
        <Require feature="pubsub-2">
            <Param name="topics">
                <![CDATA[
                    <Topic
description="Subscribes to random number generator."
name="org.apache.shindig.random-number"
                                subscribe="true"
                                title="Random Number"
                                type="number"
                    />
                ]]>
            </Param>
        </Require>
    </ModulePrefs>
    <Content type="html">
      <![CDATA[
        <script>
          var subId;
gadgets.HubSettings.params.HubClient.onSecurityAlert =
    function(alertSource, alertType) {
            alert('Security error!');
```

```
                    window.location.href = 'about:blank';
};
function callback(topic, data, subscriberData)
{                                    document.getElementById('output').
innerHTML = 'Message: ' + gadgets.util.escapeString(data + '') + '<br />' +
'Received: ' + (new Date()).toString();
}
function subscribe() {
     subId = gadgets.Hub.subscribe('org.apache.shindig.random-number',
     callback);
}
function unsubscribe() {
     gadgets.Hub.unsubscribe(subId);
document.getElementById('output').innerHTML = '';
}
     </script>
     <div>
                    <input onclick="subscribe();" type="button"
                    value="Subscribe" />
                         <input onclick="unsubscribe();" type="button"
                         value="Unsubscribe" />
     </div>
     <div id="output">
     </div>
          ]]>
     </Content>
</Module>
```

HCL

HCL Technologies Limited (formerly Hindustan Computers Limited) is an Indian IT services and consulting company, based in Noida, a satellite city of the capital Delhi.

History

In 1976, shortly after Microsoft or Apple, a group of eight engineers in India started a company to make personal computers. After an initially proposed name of Microcomp (which may have caused naming problems with Microsoft) on August 11, 1976, the company was renamed to Hindustan Computers Limited (HCL).

The company was initially focussed on hardware, but through HCL Technologies, the focus more and more became software and services.

On December 7, 2018, HCL announced an agreement under which HCL Technologies acquired certain IBM software products for $1.8 billion, including AppScan, BigFix, Commerce, Connections, Digital Experience (Portal and Content Manager), Notes/Domino, or Unica.

In 2022, HCL Technologies rebranded itself to HCLTech.

HCL DX

HCL Portal, formerly IBM WebSphere Portal, is part of HCL Digital Experience (DX).

Through an extension called Social Media Publisher, users of HCL DX can share their content with popular social networks. Out of the box the following networks are supported:

- Facebook
- LinkedIn
- Twitter/X

Social Media Publisher

Social Media Publisher can be used to manage social media posts for published, and if configured also draft content.

It supports both manual and automatic social media posts and can manage the life cycle of social media threads.

Table 7-1. *HCL Social Media Publisher – Features*

Social Network	Message Type	Statistics	URL Addressable	User Tracking	Untrack	Delete
Facebook	Page wall post	Like, comment count	Yes	Yes	Yes	Yes
Facebook	Profile posts	Like, comment count	Yes	Yes	Yes	Yes
LinkedIn	Network update	None	No	No	Yes	No
LinkedIn	Share	None	No	No	Yes	No
Twitter	Tweet	Reshare count	Yes	Yes	Yes	Yes

Settings for Facebook

Take the following steps to set up a social network connection for Facebook.

To get Facebook credentials:

1. Go to `https://developers.facebook.com/apps/`.

2. Click ***Create new App***.

3. Enter the values for the following parameters:

    a) Display name – The name of your application that is displayed at the end of each post, for example, your company name.

    b) Namespace – Optional value that is used to access Facebook Insights. It is recommended to use a unique name for each application you set up.

    c) Category – A category matching your business type. If unsure, select ***Apps for Pages***.

4. Click ***Create App***.

5. You get to a configuration screen for your application. Select *Settings* and enter the following:

    a) App domain – A comma-separated list of domains or IP addresses you want to use for this application with individual Facebook accounts. You are able to authorize your application from one of the domains/addresses in that list.

6. Click *Add Platform* and select *Website*.

7. Set *Site URL* and (if applicable) *Mobile Site URL* to the desired website, for example, http://www.mysite.com.

8. Click *Save Changes*.

9. Now you see the *App ID/API Key* and *App Secret* for your application.

Now create a new *Credential Vault* in the HCL Portal administration view where

- The *App ID/API Key* is specified as a shared *user ID*.

- The *App Secret* is specified as the *shared password*.

Then you create a social network configuration for Facebook:

1. Select *Facebook* as the social network.

2. Define authentication settings for that social network:

    a) Select the *Credential Vault* containing your Facebook credentials.

    b) Click *Authorize* to bind the credentials to a specific Facebook account.

3. Select a message type:

    - **Page wall post**

        - Select a page.

        - Enter a default name, description, image, caption, and message template. Predefined values are included as a guide, for example:

            - Name – This is posted as text.

              ```
              [Property field="title" context="current"
              type="content" format="length:100"]
              ```

- Description – This is posted as text.

  ```
  [Property field="description" context="current"
  type="content" format="length:100"]
  ```

- Image – This is posted as a URL.

  ```
  [Element context="current" type="content"
  key="Image" format="URL"]
  ```

- Caption – This is posted as text.

  ```
  [Property field="description" context="current"
  type="content" format="length:100"]
  ```

- Message – This is posted as text.

  ```
  [Element context="current" type="content"
  key="Message" format="length:100"]
  ```

- **Profile wall post**

- Select the appropriate visibility

- Enter a default name, description, image, caption, and message template. Predefined values are included as a guide. For example:

  - Name – This is posted as text.

    ```
    [Property field="title" context="current"
    type="content" format="length:100"]
    ```

  - Description – This is posted as text.

    ```
    [Property field="description" context="current"
    type="content" format="length:100"]
    ```

  - Image – This is posted as a URL.

    ```
    [Element context="current" type="content"
    key="Image" format="URL"]
    ```

  - Caption – This is posted as text.

    ```
    [Property field="description" context="current"
    type="content" format="length:100"]
    ```

- Message – This is posted as text.

```
[Element context="current" type="content"
key="Message" format="length:100"]
```

Publishing Content Directly to a Facebook Page

The Social Media Publisher is used to post status updates of your content to Facebook, but you can also post content directly to a Facebook page.

1. Go to https://developers.facebook.com/apps.

2. Click **Create new App**.

3. A form opens. Enter values for the following parameters:

   - App name – This is the name of your application that is displayed at the end of each post, for example, your company name.

   - App namespace – The name used to access Facebook Insights. It is recommended to use a unique name for each application.

4. Click **Continue**.

5. A configuration screen for your application is displayed. Select **Page Tab** under **Select how your app integrates with Facebook** and complete the following parameters:

   - Page tab name – Enter the name for the page tab.

   - Page tab URL – This is the URL to the content item you want to add to the Facebook page.

   - Secured Page tab URL – This is an https version of the Page tab URL.

6. Click **Save Changes**.

7. Click **Authorize** to bind the credentials to a specific social network account.

8. To post your content to the Facebook page, use the following URL where APP_ID is the Application ID of a Facebook Page Tab application:

```
http://www.facebook.com/dialog/pagetab?app_
id=APP_ID&next=https%3A%2F%2Fwww.facebook.
com%2Fconnect%2Flogin_success.html
```

9. Publishing content directly to a Facebook page requires a secure page tab URL. This means your server must be SSL enabled.

Settings for LinkedIn

Perform the following steps to set up a social network connection for LinkedIn.
   To get LinkedIn credentials:

1. Go to `www.linkedin.com/developers/apps`.

2. Sign in if you're not logged in yet.

3. Click **Create app**.

4. If you already have a **Company Page**, either select an existing company or select **New Company** and enter the company information.

5. Under **Create an app**, enter values for the following parameters:

   - App name – This is the name of your application that is displayed at the end of each post, for example, your company name.

   - LinkedIn page – This is the Company Page you created earlier, for example, `https://linkedin.com/company/123456`.

   - Privacy policy URL – Link to your privacy policy (optional), for example, `http://www.mysite.com/privacy`.

   - App logo – The logo is displayed to users when they authorize with your app, ideally a square image.

   - Legal agreement – Check that you have read and agree to these terms.

6. Click on **Create app**.

7. In the **Auth** tab, you'll find the **Application credentials** API Key and Client Secret. Click the "Eye" button to reveal the client secret. Record these values and fill out other settings where appropriate.

Then create a new ***Credential Vault*** in the HCL Portal administration view where

- The Client ID is specified as the shared user ID

- The Client Secret is specified as the shared password

To create a social network configuration for LinkedIn:

1. Select **LinkedIn** as the social network.

2. Define authentication settings for the social network:

    - Select the **Credential Vault** that contains your LinkedIn application credentials.

    - Click **Authorize** to bind the credentials to a specific social network account.

3. Select a message type.

    Note: It is not recommended to reference rich text elements or HTML elements in any fields that do not support HTML.

    - **Network update**

    - Enter a default message template. Predefined values are included as a guide. For example:

        - Message – This is posted as HTML.

            ```
            [Element context="current" type="content"
            key="Message" format="length:200"]
            ```

        - ```
          [URLCmpnt context="current" type="content" mode="standalone"
          start="<a href='" end="'>Link</a>"]
          ```

    - **Share**

        - Select the appropriate visibility.

        - Enter a default name, description, image, and message template. Predefined values are included as a guide. For example:
          ```

- Name – This is posted as text.

  ```
  [Property field="title" context="current"
  type="content" format="length:100"]
  ```

- Description – This is posted as text.

  ```
  [Property field="description" context="current"
  type="content" format="length:100"]
  ```

- Image – This is posted as a URL.

  ```
  [Element context="current" type="content"
  key="Image" format="URL"]
  ```

- Message – This is posted as text.

  ```
  [Element context="current" type="content"
  key="Message" format="length:200"]
  ```

Settings for Twitter/X

Perform the following steps to set up a social network connection for Twitter/X.

TWITTER TO X MIGRATION

As Elon Musk rebrands Twitter to X, at some point, even domains like twitter.com or URLs underneath that site could be switched off and no longer work. That may affect some of the settings and steps mentioned in the following text.

You must first register a Twitter application to obtain a username and password to access the Twitter API. To register a new application for use with WCM Social Media Publisher:

1. Go to `https://dev.twitter.com`.

2. Log in and click **Create an app**.

3. Click **Add New Application**.

4. Under **Application Info**, enter values for the following parameters:

- Application name – This is the name of your application that is displayed at the end of each post, for example, your company name.

- Application description – Enter a short description of the application.

- Website – This is the URL to your website, for example, `http://www.mysite.com`.

- Callback URL – Set this to http://domain/wps/wcmsocial/servlet/oAuthCB/twitter where "domain" is your domain name.

5. Read the terms and conditions and select **I Agree**.

6. Enter the security/captcha information if required.

7. Your Consumer Key and Consumer Secret are displayed. Write them down in a safe place.

8. Click the **Settings** tab.

9. In the **Application Type** section, set the **Access** property to Read and write.

10. Click the **Update this Twitter application's settings**.

Then create a new *Credential Vault* in the HCL Portal administration view where

- The Consumer Key is specified as the shared user ID

- The Consumer Secret is specified as the shared password

To create a social network configuration for Twitter/X:

1. Select *Twitter* as the social network.

2. Define authentication settings for that social network:

   a) Select the *Credential Vault* containing your Twitter application credentials.

   b) Click *Authorize* to bind the credentials to a specific social network account.

3. Enter a default message template. This is posted as text. Predefined
    tags for the message are included as a guide. For example:

```
[Property field="title" context="current" type="content"
format="length:100"]
[URLCmpnt context="current" type="content" mode="storable"]
[profilecmpnt type="content" context="current" field="keywords"
separator=" #" include="exact" start="#"]
```

Note   Rich Text is not supported for Twitter posts, so it is not recommended to reference rich text elements in your post message.

CoreMedia

While CoreMedia does not implement the Java Portlet standard, it runs on Java and is commonly used for creating "Enterprise Portals."

History

CoreMedia was founded in 1996 as a spin-off from the Multidisciplinary Engineering Science and Technology, a bit like Sun Microsystems founded at Stanford University. The company has its US HQ in Arlington, Virginia, and additional offices in Washington DC and London.

In 2012, CoreMedia introduced Elastic Social, an extension module with social interaction capabilities like content moderation, user management, etc., mimicking social networks, but not integrating them.

Social Media Hub

Unlike Elastic Social, CoreMedia Social Media Hub allows the integration of various social networks into CoreMedia Studio. It shows a separate tab with different social media feeds and messages that are to be published.

It is considered a CoreMedia Labs Blueprint or prototype that does not expose a stable API, but well, the Twitter API Client Library for Java is also in constant beta after all these years, even in version 2.x.

Installation

- From the CoreMedia application workspace, clone the repository
  `https://github.com/CoreMedia/coremedia-social-hub.git` as
  a submodule of the extensions folder. Make sure to use the branch
  name that matches your workspace version:

  ```
  git submodule add -b 1907.1 https://github.com/
  CoreMedia/coremedia-social-hub modules/extensions/
  coremedia-social-hub
  ```

- Use the extension tool in the root folder of the project to link the
  modules to your workspace:

  ```
  mvn -f workspace-configuration/extensions com.
  coremedia.maven:extensions-maven-plugin:LATEST:
  sync -Denable=coremedia-social-hub
  ```

Configuration

The configuration of Social Media Hub consists of different settings that can be applied
to global or site-specific folders.

- Global: `/Settings/Options/Settings/Social Hub/`

- Site specific: `<SITE>/Options/Settings/Social Hub/`

Global Settings

The Settings document declares global settings for the Social Media Hub and must be
located in the global settings folder. It defines credentials for a **bitly** account that is used
for link shortening, and it defines additional CAE and document type model information
that is required when media should be extracted from content for social media posts.

```
<CMSettings folder="/Settings/Options/Settings/Social Hub/"
name="Settings">
  <locale></locale>
  <master/>
  <settings>
    <Struct xmlns="http://www.coremedia.com/2008/struct">
```

```
      <StringProperty Name="bitlyUserId"></StringProperty>
      <StringProperty Name="bitlyApiKey"></StringProperty>
      <StructProperty Name="mediaMapping">
        <Struct>
          <StringProperty Name="CMMedia">data</StringProperty>
        </Struct>
      </StructProperty>
      <StringProperty Name="liveCaeUrl">YOUR_LIVE_CAE</StringProperty>
    </Struct>
  </settings>
  <identifier></identifier>
</CMSettings>
```

Media Mapping

The mediaMapping struct configures content types and property fields holding blob data that can be pushed to a social network. By default, the CoreMedia Blueprint document type model is configured for CMMedia, its data property containing a blob with asset data.

Adapter Settings

A Social Media Hub adapter configuration can be placed into the global or site-specific configuration folder.

General Adapter Settings

Every Social Media Hub adapter configuration has this structure:

```
<CMSettings folder="/Settings/Options/Settings/Social Hub/" name="My Social
Hub Adapter">
  <locale></locale>
  <master/>
  <settings>
    <Struct xmlns="http://www.coremedia.com/2008/struct">
    <StructListProperty Name="channels">
      <Struct>
        <StringProperty Name="id">ADAPTER_ID</StringProperty>
```

```
    <StringProperty Name="type">ADAPTER_TYPE</StringProperty>
    <StringProperty Name="displayName">MY ADAPTER NAME</StringProperty>
    <BooleanProperty Name="enabled">true</BooleanProperty>
    <StructProperty Name="connector">
      <Struct>
        ...
      </Struct>
    </StructProperty>
     <StructProperty Name="adapter">
      <Struct>
        ...
      </Struct>
    </StructProperty>
    </Struct>
  </StructListProperty>
  </Struct></settings>
  <identifier></identifier>
</CMSettings>
```

Every connection struct contains the properties shown in Table 7-2.

Table 7-2. *Connection Struct Properties*

Property	Description
id	The unique id of the adapter, ensure that no other adapter has the same
type	The type of the adapter
displayName	The name displayed as title in the adapter column
enabled	If the adapter is enabled or disabled
connector	Additional properties used to configure the connector of the adapter
adapter	Additional properties used to configure the adapter

When the configurations are read during startup, the Social Media Hub will try to map each configuration to the corresponding Social Media Hub adapter. It uses the implementation of SocialHubAdapterFactory available for every Social Media Hub adapter. The SocialHubAdapterFactory#getType must match the type property in the adapter setting.

Connector Settings

A connector configuration usually contains the credentials for accessing a social network or API. Apps mapping this configuration must extend the interface ConnectorConfiguration, which contains additional settings valid for all connector configurations.

The ConnectorConfiguration interface exposes the following method:

- getImageVariant() – The name of the image variant used when an image is pushed to the external system. If the variant is not found or not configured, the original blob will be used.

Twitter/X

The following section describes configuration properties for the Twitter Social Media Hub adapter.

Adapter Configuration

To show the Twitter timeline for the configured profile, the timeline link must be provided by the adapter configuration:

```
<StructProperty Name="adapter">
  <Struct>
    <StringProperty Name="timeline">https://twitter.com/[YOUR_PROFILE]</
    StringProperty>
  </Struct>
</StructProperty>
```

Connector Configuration

Create your Twitter/X application as instructed in the previous section for HCL Portal.

To use the native Twitter connector, the corresponding Twitter credentials have to be provided in the connector configuration:

```
<StructProperty Name="connector">
  <Struct>
    <StringProperty Name="consumerKey"></StringProperty>
    <StringProperty Name="consumerSecret"></StringProperty>
    <StringProperty Name="accessToken"></StringProperty>
    <StringProperty Name="accessTokenSecret"></StringProperty>
  </Struct>
</StructProperty>
```

YouTube

The following section describes configuration properties for YouTube.

Adapter Configuration
Not required

Connector Configuration
To use the native YouTube connector, you need to provide the corresponding YouTube credentials as part of the connector configuration. Note that one YouTube configuration represents one playlist. If you want to publish into different playlists, you need different configurations.

See `https://developers.google.com/youtube/v3/quickstart/go` to create YouTube credentials for your application.

```
<StructProperty Name="connector">
  <Struct>
    <StringProperty Name="credentialsJson"></StringProperty>
    <StringProperty Name="channelId"></StringProperty>
    <StringProperty Name="playlistId"></StringProperty>
  </Struct>
</StructProperty>
```

Instagram

The following section describes configuration properties for Instagram.

Adapter Configuration

Not required

Connector Configuration

Since the Social Media Hub currently does not ship a native connector for Instagram, the actual connector configuration depends on the integration with a social media tool.

Pinterest

The following section describes configuration properties for Pinterest.

Adapter Configuration

To show a Pinterest board for the configured profile, the board link must be provided in the adapter configuration. The link can be copied from your Pinterest profile:

```
<StructProperty Name="adapter">
  <Struct>
    <StringProperty Name="board">https://www.pinterest.de/[PINTEREST_
    PRROFILE]/[PINTEREST_BOARD_NAME]</StringProperty>
  </Struct>
</StructProperty>
```

Connector Configuration

Since the Social Media Hub currently does not ship a native connector for this social network, the actual connector configuration depends on the integration with a social media tool.

Summary

In this final chapter, we learned about Enterprise Portal servers and their social media support, either by providing social interactions within the portal itself or by integrating social networks, from using them for social login to sharing content or embedding the social timelines.

References

1. Wikipedia – Agora: http://en.wikipedia.org/wiki/Agora

2. Wikipedia – Forum: http://en.wikipedia.org/wiki/Forum_(Roman)

3. History of Information – Wikis/Forum Posts: www.historyofinformation.com/expanded.php?category=Social+Media+%2F+Social+Networks+%2F+Wikis

4. The Role of Social Media in Political Mobilisation, dissertation by Madeline Storck, December 20, 2011: www.culturaldiplomacy.org/academy/content/pdf/participant-papers/2012-02-bifef/The_Role_of_Social_Media_in_Political_Mobilisation_-_Madeline_Storck.pdf

5. Wikipedia – Agorism: http://en.wikipedia.org/wiki/Agorism

6. Wikipedia – Six Degrees: http://en.wikipedia.org/wiki/Six_degrees

7. Reuters – Mt. Gox files for bankruptcy, hit with lawsuit: www.reuters.com/article/us-bitcoin-mtgox-bankruptcy-idUSBREA1ROFX20140228

8. Wikipedia – Friend of a Friend: http://en.wikipedia.org/wiki/FOAF_(software)

9. Wikipedia – RSS: http://en.wikipedia.org/wiki/RSS

10. Wikipedia – Aaron Swartz' A Programmable Web: An Unfinished Work, Copyright © 2013 by Morgan & Claypool: http://upload.wikimedia.org/wikipedia/commons/3/3f/Aaron_Swartz_s_A_Programmable_Web_An_Unfinished_Work.pdf

11. Java Community Process: https://jcp.org

© Werner Keil 2024
W. Keil, *Enterprise Social for the Java Platform*, https://doi.org/10.1007/978-1-4842-9571-7

REFERENCES

12. Wikipedia – Mashup: `http://en.wikipedia.org/wiki/Mashup_(web_application_hybrid)`

13. Wikipedia – BEA AquaLogic: `https://en.wikipedia.org/wiki/BEA_Systems#AquaLogic`

14. What are Walled Gardens? The Definitive 2023 Guide: `https://www.kevel.com/blog/what-are-walled-gardens`

15. Wikipedia – Open Social: `http://en.wikipedia.org/wiki/OpenSocial`

16. ZDNet – How we can create open standards for social business by Dion Hinchcliffe: `https://www.zdnet.com/article/how-we-can-create-open-standards-for-social-business/`

17. Wikipedia – List of social networking services: `https://en.wikipedia.org/wiki/List_of_social_networking_services`

18. Twitter4J: `https://twitter4j.org/`
    GitHub: `https://github.com/Twitter4J/Twitter4J`

19. Apache Shindig: `http://shindig.apache.org/`

20. OSDE – Google Code: `https://code.google.com/p/opensocial-development-environment/`

21. Glassfish SocialSite Developer's Guide: `https://docs.oracle.com/cd/E19957-01/820-6356/820-6356.pdf`

22. SlideShare – DaliCore: `www.slideshare.net/johanvanstichel/dalicore-5313314`

23. Wikipedia – List of Acquisitions by Oracle: `http://en.wikipedia.org/wiki/List_of_acquisitions_by_Oracle`

24. Using Oracle Social Network: `https://docs.oracle.com/cloud/latest/related-docs/OSNUG/toc.htm`

25. Spring Social: `https://spring.io/projects/spring-social`

26. Social Media JSR 357 rejected by Java Community Process: www.h-online.com/open/news/item/Social-Media-JSR-357-rejected-by-Java-Community-Process-1478310.html

27. Wikipedia – Principle of least privilege: http://en.wikipedia.org/wiki/Principle_of_least_privilege

28. Jakarta Contexts and Dependency Injection: https://jakarta.ee/specifications/cdi/

29. OpenID: https://openid.net/

30. W3C SocialWG: www.w3.org/Social/WG

31. OPENi: https://cordis.europa.eu/project/id/317883

32. Jakarta Security: https://jakarta.ee/specifications/security/

33. Agorava Project: https://agorava.github.io

34. Microsoft Embedded Social: www.microsoft.com/en-us/research/project/microsoft-embedded-social/
GitHub: https://github.com/microsoft/EmbeddedSocial-Java-API-Library

35. Twitter API Client Library for Java: https://github.com/twitterdev/twitter-api-java-sdk

36. Meta Business SDK: https://developers.facebook.com/docs/business-sdk
GitHub (for Java): https://github.com/facebook/facebook-java-business-sdk

37. Wikipedia – Privacy concerns with social networking: http://en.wikipedia.org/wiki/Privacy_concerns_with_social_networking_services

38. Can Social Media Solve Boris Nemtsov's Murder? https://socialmedianyu.wordpress.com/2015/03/03/can-social-media-solve-boris-nemtsovs-murder/

REFERENCES

39. AP News – Germany's telegram era ends with final rush of thousands: https://apnews.com/article/germany-business-d3 bbbebe521049fc99bee29310104ad8

40. YouTube – Me at the zoo: https://youtu.be/jNQXAC9IVRw

41. Wikipedia – Andreas Kaplan: https://en.wikipedia.org/wiki/ Andreas_Kaplan

42. Wikipedia – List of mergers and acquisitions by Microsoft: https://en.wikipedia.org/wiki/List_of_mergers_and_ acquisitions_by_Microsoft

43. Verizon is selling Tumblr to WordPress' owner: www.theverge. com/2019/8/12/20802639/tumblr-verizon-sold-wordpress- blogging-yahoo-adult-content

44. Wikipedia – 2020 Twitter account hijacking: https:// en.wikipedia.org/wiki/2020_Twitter_account_hijacking

45. Trump's Social Media Site Quietly Admits It's Based on Mastodon: https://uk.pcmag.com/social-media/137421/trumps-social- media-site-quietly-admits-its-based-on-mastodon

46. Kanye West isn't buying Parler after all: https://techcrunch. com/2022/12/01/kanye-west-isnt-buying-parler-after-all

47. SFMOMA – 1997: Birth of the Camera Phone: www.sfmoma.org/ watch/1997-birth-of-the-camera-phone-2/

48. JSR 168 – Portlet Specification: www.jcp.org/en/jsr/ detail?id=168

49. Metaverse Post – ChatGPT passes the Turing test: https://mpost. io/chatgpt-passes-the-turing-test/

50. TechCrunch – Twitter Suddenly Locks Thousands of Accounts: http://techcrunch.com/2015/02/10/twitter-account-locked/

51. Fitbit is getting rid of the best reasons to use a Fitbit, which is a big mistake: www.xda-developers.com/fitbit-ending-challenges- adventures-big-mistake/

52. Parler's New Owner Shuts Down Site: `www.techdirt.com/2023/04/17/parlers-new-owner-shuts-down-site-no-reasonable-person-believes-twitter-for-conservatives-is-a-viable-business-model/`

53. CNN – DeSantis' Twitter launch disaster shows Musk's platform isn't ready for prime time: `https://edition.cnn.com/2023/05/25/media/desantis-twitter-musk-reliable-sources/index.html`

54. CNBC – Reddit will charge hefty fees to the many third-party apps that access its data: `www.cnbc.com/2023/06/01/reddit-eyeing-ipo-charge-millions-in-fees-for-third-party-api-access.html`

55. IEEE Xplore – A Comparison of Commercial and Military Computer Security Policies: `https://ieeexplore.ieee.org/document/6234890`

56. JBoss Community Archive – Agorava: `https://docs.jboss.org/author/display/AGOVA/`

57. Reuters – Meta's Threads swiftly signs up 30 million users: `www.reuters.com/technology/metas-threads-is-true-threat-musk-owned-twitter-analysts-say-2023-07-06/`

58. Wired – X Isn't a Super App. It's Just Twitter: `www.wired.com/story/twitter-x-rebrand-elon-musk/`

59. WhatsApp Business Java API SDK: `https://bindambc.github.io/whatsapp-business-java-api/`

60. GNU social: `https://gnusocial.network/`

61. Mastodon: `https://joinmastodon.org/`

62. Friendica: `https://friendi.ca/`

63. W3C Social Web Protocols: `www.w3.org/TR/social-web-protocols/`

64. Observer - Meta is Reportedly the Latest Social Media Company to Embrace ActivityPub Technology: `https://observer.com/2023/03/meta-is-reportedly-the-latest-social-media-company-to-embrace-activitypub-technology/`

65. Matrix: `https://matrix.org/`

66. Keycloak: `www.keycloak.org/`

67. Spring Security: `https://spring.io/projects/spring-security`

68. Micronaut: `https://micronaut.io/`

Index

A

Access control, 74, 93
Activity API, 33
ActivityPub, 38, 40–44, 46
ActivityStreams, 41–43
Agorava
    connectors, 245
    core, 242, 243
    definition, 239
    history, 239
    macro architecture, 240–242
    PicketLink, 243, 244
    socializer, 245, 246
Amazon, 3, 6, 9, 14, 57
Apache Shindig, 35, 55–57, 264
Apache Shiro
    application developers, 161
    definition, 161
    features, 163, 164
        authentication, 164, 165
        authorization, 166, 167
        session management, 169
    framework, 161
    realm, 163
    SecurityManager, 162
    social login, 170, 171, 173–179
    subject, 162
Apple Health, 21, 22
Attribute-based access control
        (ABAC), 142
Audiobooks, 14
Audio sharing, 13

B

Batch Mode, 195, 256
BigBone, 204
Big Data, 40

C

ChatGPT, 7, 8
Common Client Interface (CCI), 241, 242
Confidentiality, 63, 64, 240
Context-based access control (CBAC), 142
CoreMedia
    history, 276
    social media hub
        configuration, 277, 278, 280–282
        installation, 277
CoreMedia Labs Blueprint, 276
COVID-19 pandemic, 7
Cryptography, 169
@CustomFormAuthenticationMechanism
        Definition annotation, 114
Cybersecurity attacks, 63

D

Diaspora, 46, 68
Digital Business Cards, 37

Authentication, 57, 64, 69, 71–74, 78–91,
        113–117, 137–142, 153–154,
        158–160, 234–235
Authorization, 64, 74–75, 142, 166–169, 220

© Werner Keil 2024
W. Keil, *Enterprise Social for the Java Platform*, https://doi.org/10.1007/978-1-4842-9571-7

Printed in the United States
by Baker & Taylor Publisher Services